Anne Martin

Rooted in the *Divine*

Nurturing Our Faith through Small Group Ministry

The United Church of Canada

Rooted in the Divine
Nurturing Our Faith through Small Group Ministry

By Anne Martin

Copyright © 2004
The United Church of Canada

All biblical quotations, unless otherwise noted, are from the New Revised Standard Version Bible, copyright © 1989, by the Division of Christian Education of the National Council of the Churches of Christ in the United States of America. Used by permission.

Care has been taken to trace ownership of copyright material contained in this text. The publisher will gratefully accept any information that will enable it to rectify any reference or credit in subsequent printings.

ISBN: 1-55134-133-6

The United Church of Canada
3250 Bloor St. West, Suite 300
Toronto, ON   M8X 2Y4
Canada
416-231-5931
www.united-church.ca

Design and Production: Carina Cruz, Graphics and Print
Cover Photo: Bill Bachman/Getty Images

Printed in Canada

5   4   3   2   1   07   06   05   04   03

030349

I am the vine, you are the branches.
Those who abide in me and I in them bear much fruit...
John 15:5

Acknowledgements

This book would not have been possible without support from the former
Division of Mission in Canada and The United Church of Canada's General
Council units: Support to Local Ministries, Faith Formation and Education, and
Resource, Production, and Distribution. Many thanks to the many people who
took the time to read and critique the book in its various stages of development.
A special thanks to Annie Roper who created the vine image and to all those whose
wisdom and patience helped to see the project through.

Anne Martin

Contents

Introduction 6

Part I: Thinking About Small Group Ministry
    1. What is Small Group Ministry?....................12
    2. The Vine Image of Small Group Ministry 18
    3. Why Small Group Ministry? 21
    4. Developing Core Values for Small Group Ministry 23

Part II: Putting Small Group Ministry into Practice
    5. Getting Started 30
    6. The Meeting space....................................35
    7. The Small Group Meeting.........................37
    8. The Group Covenant................................46
    9. Facilitating Small Groups.........................53
    10. Examples of Small Groups 57
    11. Prayer and Spiritual Discipline Groups 62
    12. Considering the Group's Ministry 70

Appendix 1:
Options for Openings, Check-Ins, Closings, and Check-Outs 72

Appendix 2:
Some Questions about Small Group Ministry 78

Bibliography 81

> *Spiritual life is a journey.*
> *Small group ministry is an invitation to journey together,*
> *travelling to places hitherto unknown.*

Introduction

> *The individual is a pilgrim who is journeying to a place where the*
> *divine and the human meet.*

John Welch[1]

Living Out Our Call

As participants in The United Church of Canada, we are called

> *to celebrate God's presence,*
> *to live with respect in Creation,*
> *to love and serve others,*
> *to seek justice and resist evil,*
> *to proclaim Jesus, crucified and risen,*
> > *our judge and our hope.*

From "A New Creed"

In answer to that call, we gather together. We form congregations, assemblies of people, gatherings to witness to our faith and to find support to live out our ministry and mission. Most congregations come together weekly to celebrate God's presence through worship.

The experience of congregational worship is important. For many people, however, to grow in understanding of what it means to be in community with God and with others, congregational worship is not enough. Many people also look for opportunities to:

❖ explore their spirituality and deepen their faith in an environment where they can feel free to share their experiences, doubts, and fears;

❖ come together with others for support and fellowship;

❖ study the Bible and the Christian tradition without having doctrines "laid on";

❖ learn how to pray and to develop spiritual practices;

---

[1] Excerpt from *Spiritual Pilgrims: Carl Jung and Teresa of Avila*, by John Welch, Copyright © 1982, Paulist Press, Inc., New York/Mahwah, N.J., p. 16. Used with permission of Paulist Press.

❖ be challenged to grow in their understanding of self, God, and others;

❖ engage with and challenge their faith community;

❖ find ways to live out their faith more fully so they can make a difference in the world by seeking justice and resisting evil.

Small group ministry offers participants the chance to fulfill some of these needs. *Rooted in the Divine* is intended to help congregations in this endeavour by providing an overview of small group ministry and practical ways to carry it out.

Why This Resource?

This resource has five key purposes:

1. to provide a small group ministry resource that encourages different theological perspectives;

2. to support spiritual nurture in the church through prayer and other spiritual practices;

3. to provide an opportunity to journey with others;

4. to welcome participants, as they are, into small groups;

5. to help congregations be open to the Spirit's creative demands for developing community.

Encouraging Different Theological Perspectives

The small group ministry process encourages a deepening relationship with God and with community as participants engage in their faith journeys. Participants in the small group process will have many different theological perspectives. Along the way there may be transformative moments, profound "Aha!" moments, as well as the occasional "Oh no!" moment. Participants may experience an overwhelming new awareness that seems to turn them inside out, to "convert" them to a new way of being. The goal of the journey, however, is not to reach a particular endpoint to reach a definitive theological perspective, at which one can say, "I'm here. I've made it!" Rather, the goal is an ever-deepening experience of what it means to know God, to be in community, and to seek justice in a broken world.

Encouraging Spiritual Nurture

Rooted in the Divine encourages spiritual nurture—that is, it encourages participants to deepen their relationship with God, to become "rooted in the Divine." As communities of faith, United Church congregations have the obligation to offer people seeking a relationship with God ways in which to do that. Since prayer is fundamental to developing one's relationship with God, developing a prayer life is essential.

Each small group is therefore asked to spend time together in prayer or some other spiritual practice. Through this ongoing process the faith life of the participants, the groups, and the congregation as a whole is nurtured and supported.

Note: In *Rooted in the Divine*, "spirituality" refers to acknowledging and pursuing a relationship with God. "Faith" refers to the deepening assurance that one experiences as one engages in the spiritual quest.

Journeying with Others

Personal faith journeys are just that, *personal* faith journeys. Paradoxically, personal faith journeys are never carried out alone. Whether we recognize it or not, we are always journeying with God. "We are not alone; we live in God's world." God is ever-present.

We are also always journeying with others. We make our way through life in community. Small group ministry provides the opportunity to join with others, to discover what it means to be part of God's creation, and to be challenged to respond to creation with compassion and justice as members of the faith community.

Welcoming Participants as They Are

We live in a time of deep spiritual hunger. While many people in our society have no formal religious background, they still yearn for a relationship with God and for a community within which they can live out their faith journeys and make sense of their personal experiences.

Participating in small group ministry means accepting the invitation to come "as you are," wherever you happen to be on your personal faith journey.

Participants, however, do not come empty-handed. They bring with them their own gifts, interests, and yearnings; a variety of life experiences, both joyous and painful; their personal understanding of scripture, or perhaps lack of it, and a desire to live more fully. They also bring the hard questions that arise from the day-to-day world in which they live—questions that may both confirm and challenge their faith.

To make small group ministry meaningful, congregations must be open to welcoming everyone who struggles with faith questions and wants a deeper understanding of faith and spirituality, regardless of where they are on their own faith journeys.

Developing Community

In *The Practice of Prayer*, Margaret Guenther writes, "If we are to grow up into Christ, we must be willing to push out the boundaries and accept the possibility of change—not change in the immutable God who was and is, but change in our perception and understanding of who this God is and who we are in relationship to God."[2] *Rooted in the Divine* is about accepting this challenge to grow in response to "God who was and is."

To grow one must hunger and thirst and want to be satisfied. As we learn to rest more and more in God's love, we find our hunger is never fully satisfied. As we grow in God, we long to grow more deeply in God to set our roots ever deeper. Small group ministry offers all who are spiritually thirsty and hungry the opportunity to experience a community that can help feed them as they journey together in response to God's love and grace.

> *As the deer longs for flowing streams, so my soul longs for you, O God.*
>
> Psalm 42:1

While visiting a Trappist monastery, writer and educator Parker Palmer realized "true community arises not from our own social graces but from the mediation of God's grace among us.... I do not suggest that the congregation should become a monastery, but only that we find ways of adapting this key insight of monastic life."[3] Palmer recognizes the importance of the church as a place where strangers meet on safe ground: the ground of common commitment. He recognizes that, to some degree, we are strangers to one another as well as to ourselves. Small group participants journey together, known but also strangers on a quest. Acknowledging God's presence, they learn to allow God to mediate among them, thereby experiencing God's grace through their commitment to one another.

Who This Resource Is For

This resource is for those who are concerned about the spiritual nurture of people in their congregation.

Small group ministry is not simply about having small groups as part of the congregation. It has to do with an alternative way of being a congregation in

---

[2] Margaret Guenther, *The Practice of Prayer* (Cambridge, MA: Cowley, 1998), p. 16. Used by permission.

[3] Parker Palmer, *The Company of Strangers: Christians and the Renewal of America's Public Life* (New York: Crossroad, 1983), pp. 133–34. Used by permission.

response to God's call to love God and to be in relation with one another.

If small group ministry is to develop within a congregation in a significant way, it has to be a joint undertaking of the congregation and its clergy, focused together on what the Spirit is doing in their midst, and finding ways to respond.

Using *Rooted in the Divine*

Rooted in the Divine is divided into two parts. Part I: Thinking About Small Group Ministry (chapters 1–5) provides the "theory" of small group ministry, the "what is it all about?" Part II: Putting Small Group Ministry into Practice (chapters 6–16) is the "how-to."

It is important to spend some time going through Part I to consider what small group ministry is all about before jumping in. One way to approach this is to bring together three to seven people to consider what small group ministry might mean for your congregation—in other words, form a small group to study small group ministry. The group would:

❖ develop a group covenant, as described in Chapter 8;

❖ follow the group process outlined in Chapter 5;

❖ spend the "group interest time" part of the process (see Chapter 5 and 7) discussing the different chapters, perhaps one at each meeting;

❖ use Praying with Scripture (Chapter 11, page 66) as a group spiritual practice.

Small group ministry is an invitation to journey together, travelling to places hitherto unknown. Welcome to the journey!

Part I
Thinking About Small Group Ministry

Chapter 1
What is Small Group Ministry?

Christian commitment is a question of fused purpose of many people gifted for mission out of their shared experience.

John Welch[4]

Small groups have long been a part of the United Church—Bible study groups, youth groups, fellowship groups, outreach groups, UCW units, choirs—the list goes on and on. So why promote small group ministry now? Is it really something new? Hasn't it been happening all along?

To begin to understand the idea of small group ministry, it is helpful to distinguish between congregations with small groups and congregations of small groups.

Congregations *with* Small Groups

Congregations *with* small groups have some or perhaps many small groups, such as those mentioned above. These groups play a significant role. While acknowledging that the people of God all engage in ministry, and that ministry certainly occurs through the work of small groups, these congregations' structures do not directly reflect this core value.

Many who take part in groups such as boards, session, councils, and various committees are often there out of a sense of duty or of having to get things done rather than out of a sense of life-giving ministry and a deepening of their faith and spirituality. Various types of groups are certainly encouraged, but leadership training that links the development of "ministry" with facilitation skills is usually not provided.

Congregations *with* small groups do not promote and nurture all small group work as a form of ministry that encourages participants to deepen their understanding of faith and spirituality, to seek justice, and to create a healthy community of faith. These congregations are not structured to reflect that all are called to ministry.

---

[4] Excerpt from *Spiritual Pilgrims: Carl Jung and Teresa of Avila*, by John Welch, Copyright © 1982, Paulist Press, Inc., New York/Mahwah, N.J., p. 133. Used with permission of Paulist Press.

Congregations *of* Small Groups

Congregations *of* small groups intentionally develop small group ministry as central to their congregational life, promote spiritual growth for their participants and consequently work toward a healthy, ministering environment. Congregations *of* small groups recognize that small group ministry provides a framework within which participants can intentionally engage in ministry as they respond to God's call to community.

Congregations *of* small groups, therefore:

❖ recognize that all "work" done within the congregation is a form of ministry and encourage members to participate according to their interests and passions;

❖ are willing to look honestly at who they are as congregations, see what is life-giving and what is not, as they seek to know God more deeply and live out of God's love to create a more just world;

❖ acknowledge the importance of prayer and other spiritual practices individually and within small groups to develop and maintain a healthy congregation;

❖ provide ongoing leadership development;

❖ offer a means for becoming more accountable to self and others;

❖ ground personal experience in a Christian framework whereby "my story" is also "our story";

❖ encourage its members to develop and share their gifts;

❖ celebrate the gifts of the community.

Small Group Ministry: A Closer Look

To understand small group ministry further let's look more closely at the name, *small group ministry.*

Small Group Ministry Refers to Small Groups

It goes without saying that the more participants a group has the greater the number of relationships within the group. For example, a group of three people results in six relationships. (Arrows represent two-way relationships.)

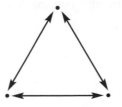

A group of six people results in 30 relationships.

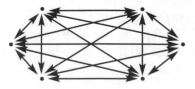

In a group of 15 participants there will be 210 relationships. Building community and developing intimate relationships become more difficult in large groups.

Small group ministry groups are therefore always small. Some groups can work well with as few as three participants. Groups of six to eight maximize the involvement of all members and create the opportunity for effective community building.

Small Group Ministry Emphasizes *Groups*

While effective small group work depends on good leadership, small group ministry stresses the group as a whole rather than "a leader" and "participants." At its best, small group ministry is a synergetic experience in which participants find a deeper understanding of self, God, and community.

The small group process helps participants develop their spirituality through whatever activity the group takes on, be that a particular interest or some aspect of the congregation's governance. If all the work of the church is seen as an opportunity to develop spiritually through the development of an interest, then all the work of the church is recognized as "holy" work. Work within the congregation is not carried out as merely a commitment or an obligation that needs to be done, often unwillingly or begrudgingly, or, unfortunately in some cases, as a way to exert personal power over others. The holy work of congregations includes boards, sessions, councils, and committees, all of which can carry out their ministries based on the small group process.

Small groups form intentional group covenants to come together for a particular purpose for a specific length of time. Participants develop a covenant that sets the guidelines for their time together. (See Chapter 8.)

Small Group Ministry is *Ministry*

Ministry is the response to God's love and the desire to live out of that love within the world. It is, therefore, experiential, relational, and transformative.

Ministry as Experiential

Individuals come into the group with their own histories and personal stories that will affect the way they participate, determine their expectations from the group, and influence the way in which they will grow spiritually.

In small group ministry, participants find a way to understand and share their personal experience of God's activity in their lives. This helps them find common ground to do ministry together.

Ministry as Relational

Personal spiritual development—growing in God's love—is experienced through relationships. Human beings are by nature relational. We are all born into a world where we depend on others in order to survive. Knowing what it is to love and to be loved depends on our relationship with others.

Ministry as a response to God's call means responding with an openness to be in "right relationship" with others. Right relationship means that there is give and take in the relationship. *Giving* means responding to the opportunity to share one's faith by living out God's call to action. As one develops in God's love, one feels more strongly the lure of God's call to action, to give of one's self.

Taking means being open to what the situation has to offer for the individual participants and for the group. Spiritual growth is never one-sided. We grow by being open to the world, by our willingness to be in relation with others and learn from them. If one only wishes to give but resists being open to the challenge of receiving what others have to offer, spiritual development will be stunted by pride and arrogance.

For example, we may minister to homeless people by providing Out of the Cold programs in our churches. We can act out of the conviction that it is God's will that all have their basic needs met which include food, shelter, and acceptance. If, however, we act out of a patronizing attitude and a need to serve our own egos, or if we act wishing to "feel good" about helping others who we deem as less fortunate than ourselves, we do not serve as Jesus calls us to serve. Yet if we act out of non-judgmental compassion and a desire to do God's will, we are closer to answering Jesus' call to service.

Jesus served others out of deeply-felt compassion. His service was grounded in the recognition that right relationship means knowing God in oneself and in others. We do those who we wish to serve a terrible *dis*service when we in fact use them to bolster ourselves. Service stems from that profound love which comes from experiencing God within ourselves, from seeing God in the other, from seeing our connectedness in this world, and from knowing, in the deepest sense of the word, what it means to say that "when one suffers, all suffer."

Small group ministry appreciates that human life is lived in relationships. It challenges us to think about how we can relate to each other in creative and life-giving ways.

Transformative

Ministry begins with the relationship between God and self. As we open ourselves to God's ministering power, we are able to love more deeply and respond out of that love. We are, therefore, challenged to deepen our own experience of God's love as well as our potential for personal and communal transformation.

Through an ever-deepening willingness to listen, appropriate disclosure, confidentiality, accountability, and support, small group ministry can help congregations grow deeper in faith and deeper in ministry as an expression of that faith.

To Whom Does Small Group Ministry Minister?

We are called to be in community with God and with others—individual people, the faith community, and the wider world.

Ministry to the Individual

Ministry begins with the individual person. As communities of faith congregations should provide spiritual nurture, opportunities for faith development, and pastoral care. These needs can be meet in many ways. Small group ministry is a way of being in relationship to nurture the participants' spiritual lives so that they can deepen their faith.

Ministry to the Faith Community

Just as everyone gains when church groups are connected with each other, lack of connection between them is a loss for everyone in the congregation. The question is, how does a congregation find ways for its groups to minister to the congregation as a whole? How does the ministry extend beyond the individual groups?

Small group ministry encourages congregations to consider their small groups as part of an interconnected whole. This can happen in various ways, such as:

❖ exploring new ways to experience congregational worship which reflect some of the small groups' experiences;

❖ providing educational opportunities for others related to the groups' interests;

❖ a congregational small group ministry newsletter, bulletin board, or Web site.

Ministry to the Wider World

Ministry goes beyond the congregation. Participants are encouraged to consider ways in which their experiences and learnings influence, and are influenced by, their relationship to the wider world. Consciousness raising, education, and commitment to challenge unjust social structures are all ways of ministering to the wider world.

Some groups may feel called to some sort of direct action. A new ministry focus may arise and a new group may wish to form around it. For others, it may be enough to reflect on the way the group learnings are impacting on the participants' personal lives.

Participants join small groups for various reasons. Some seek the fulfillment of a personal spiritual longing. Some seek a community of faith for support, and friendship. Others join small groups in response to a social justice issue. When the congregation's ministry is developed intentionally, all aspects of ministry—to individual people, to the faith community, and to the wider world—will unfold in an interrelated way, nurturing each other as the Spirit moves in and through the congregation's life.

Chapter 2
The Vine Image of Small Group Ministry

I am the real vine, and my Father is the vinegrower....
Live in me, as I in you.
A branch cannot bear fruit by itself;
it must be attached to the vine.

John 15:1, 4 (adapted)

Just like the vine that winds and grows
Every new branch brings a strength
that flows through its reaching arms
that embrace and unfold,
and the roots
grow deeper
and stronger.

Nan Thompson[5]

The vine is one image to help congregations move into a deeper understanding of what it means to develop small group ministry.

The vine image has five parts:

❖ the earth

❖ the vine

❖ the fruit of the vine

❖ the trellis

❖ the cross supports

---

[5] Nan Thompson wrote this song for a small group ministry presentation developed by the Mission and Outreach Committee of Wesley United in Cambridge, Ontario. Used with permission.

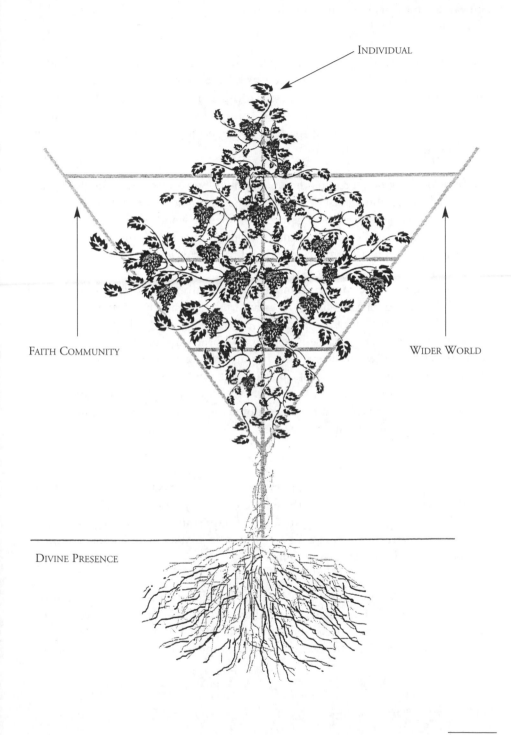

The earth represents God's presence in the world that nourishes, grounds, and sustains life.

The vine represents the congregation. The vine is rooted in the earth—in God— and relies on God's gracious love to grow as fully as possible. For a congregation to flourish, it must root itself firmly in God. It must understand the relationship between God and God's people. In other words, what do God's people need today to grow fruitfully in God? What speaks to God's people today that can lead them into God's depths and love?

The fruit of the vine represents the small groups. In this image, small groups are represented by the abundance of fruit clustered throughout the vine. Fruit does not last forever. Small groups come together for a specific length of time and then end. Once ripe, the fruit falls to the ground. It helps to nurture the soil as the congregation develops its ministry needs and more fruit emerges.

The trellis supports the congregation and its small groups. The congregation needs strong structural support to sustain its growth. As in a garden, different plants require different structures for support. The purpose of a trellis is to support the vine. The vine's primary purpose is to grow and bear fruit, not to maintain the trellis. It therefore needs to be stressed that support for the congregation must reflect congregational needs. If not, the congregation becomes "regimented" by the structure, a situation that can unfortunately stifle rather than enhance faith and spirituality as the congregation becomes more concerned with maintaining the structure and "keeping things as they are" than assessing if the way things are in fact serves its spiritual needs.

The congregation maintains itself by responding to its call to ministry. The three prongs of the trellis therefore represent the three aspects of ministry, with the individual at the centre, and with the faith community and the wider world on either side. Small group ministry provides the opportunity for congregations to structure themselves to develop each aspect of ministry, and consequently helps congregations to bear their own weight.

The cross supports represent the interconnections between these three aspects of small group ministry. The three horizontal cross supports of the trellis represent the intentional connections between individuals, the faith community, and the wider world. These connections are essential for the congregation to be well supported.

Chapter 3
Why Small Group Ministry?

... there are varieties of activities, but it is the same God who activates all of them in everyone. To each is given the manifestation of the Spirit for the common good.

1 Corinthians 12:6-7

For the congregation as a whole, small group ministry offers a number of things:

Small group ministry helps the congregation to think about and shape its life asking such questions as: What is life-giving for us? What is not life-giving? What do we feel that God is asking of us as a faith community?
When a congregation undertakes small group ministry, everyone affiliated with it is encouraged to create community with others according to their interests. Participants are asked to identify their own interests, core values, and needs, and to explore them in terms of developing their faith and spirituality. This process provides the congregation with the opportunity to explore what it means to be a community of faith and how best to live out that experience so that it is life-giving, faith-deepening, and justice-making.

Small group ministry encourages and fosters lay leadership.
Effective small group ministry not only depends on the development of lay leadership, it encourages lay leadership. Leadership development for small group ministry promotes personal growth through spiritual and faith development, and helps leaders learn effective small group skills (see Chapter 9).

Small group ministry can develop a helpful pastoral care network and reduce crisis situations for ministry personnel and lay leaders.
In groups that function well, many personal stories will be told, some of which will be about participants' personal concerns and struggles. The group is not asked to take these on as a team to solve the problems. Small groups are not therapy groups. Participants, however, can offer each other a safe place to tell their stories and support each other through listening and through prayer—through intentionally letting God be part of the relationship. In other words, groups can offer a form of pastoral care.

Parker Palmer writes, "To let God mediate our relationships means, in this case, that when one listens to another's need, one listens not with a sense of personal power to 'straighten things out' but with a sense of God's presence which alone can heal. We cannot carry the impossible burden of each other's problems. Freed from the need to 'solve' anyone's problems, we can be fully present to each other as friends, embodiments of the love God has for each of us in our need."[6]

It may be important to set boundaries around the limits of care that the group can provide. When a participant needs care that goes beyond what the group can provide, she or he may need to speak with the minister or another member of the community.

To provide pastoral care, small group ministry can offer participants:

❖ a safe environment;

❖ the opportunity to develop trust and intimacy within a group;

❖ a place to develop listening skills;

❖ accountability to each other which includes letting the group know if there is a reason to keep a participant from coming to the group, e.g. a death or illness in the family, and being honest about any concerns about the way in which the group is working;

❖ a place for personal concerns to be raised;

❖ a place to identify personal concerns that may require help from beyond the group.

Small group ministry provides an entry into the congregation for new participants while revitalizing the faith of those already affiliated with the congregation.

When newcomers make contact with a congregation, small group ministry can help them to find a way to belong. The opportunity for spiritual growth and faith development by pursuing an interest in a safe and caring environment, while at the same time challenging and inspiring, can help newcomers feel a strong sense of belonging.

Of course, not only newcomers benefit from small group ministry. Those already affiliated with a congregation find that small group ministry provides them with the opportunity for a revitalized faith and spiritual life as well as a renewed sense of what it means to belong to a faith community.

---

[6] Parker Palmer, *Company of Strangers: Christians and the Renewal of America's Public Life*, (New York: Crossroad, 1983), p. 134. Used by permission.

Chapter 4
Developing Core Values for Small Group Ministry

When introducing small group ministry, groups need to consider the values that they wish to preserve and the values that they wish to develop. Groups need to consider such questions as:

❖ What is life-giving for us?

❖ What is essential to help us develop as a community of faith?

In this chapter, Prayerful, Affirming, Challenging, Celebratory, and Safe (PACCS) small groups are discussed as one grouping of core values for developing small group ministry. These are not the only important values but are presented here as one approach that can be used to help congregations to develop their own.

Prayerful

Prayer is a process of discovering ourselves more fully in God's love.

Marjorie Thompson[7]

In small groups, participants learn to pray and to develop personal prayer lives by affirming that God is always present and accessible. Participants are united through the power of the Spirit and come to recognize that God's work for one person is for everyone. As individuals grow stronger in the Spirit, they often work through the dynamics of group building more effectively.

Prayer is fundamental to small group ministry. Many church meetings certainly incorporate prayer into their openings and closings. However, participants need more than book-ending meetings in prayer to help develop a significant prayer life.

---

[7] Reproduced from *Soul Feast: An Invitation to the Christian Spiritual Life*, by Marjorie Thompson, p. 44. © 1995 Marjorie Thompson. Used by permission of Westminster John Knox Press.

Developing prayer practices benefits not only the individual but also the whole community.

In *The Mentor's Spirit*, Marsha Sinetar says that "when the Holy Spirit acts in or through even one individual, everyone within that person's reach gets blessed, energized, more loving, healed and creatively fluent, if briefly."[8] It is therefore suggested that participants take 20-30 minutes at each meeting to pray together and to develop a variety of approaches to prayer and other spiritual disciplines.

Accepting and Affirming

Wisdom begins when we take things as they are; otherwise we get nowhere.

Carl Jung[9]

Encouraging the value of acceptance and affirmation allows the participants to feel free to be themselves and to accept each other as they are at this time. The experiences that participants bring to the group encourage participation and growth as they build a community of trust, integrity, and openness.

Accepting means saying "yes" to each other, affirming participants as they are at the moment. Participants go into groups not expecting themselves or others to change, although this might happen, but simply to be part of the group, journeying together, discovering ways to be more rooted in the Divine. By accepting one another for who they are, participants create the space for spiritual growth for themselves and others.

In *Anam Cara*, John O'Donohue writes, "Every person has certain qualities or presences in their heart that are awkward, disturbing and negative. One of your sacred duties is to exercise kindness toward them. In a sense you are called to be a loving parent to your delinquent qualities."[10]

---

[8] Marsha Sinetar, *The Mentor's Spirit: Life Lessons on Leadership and the Art of Encouragement*, (New York: St. Martin's Press, 1998), p. 144. Used by permission.

[9] Excerpt from *Spiritual Pilgrims: Carl Jung and Teresa of Avila*, by John Welch, Copyright © 1982, Paulist Press, Inc. New York/Mahwah, N.J., p. 118. Used with permission of Paulist Press.

[10] *Anam Cara: A Book of Celtic Wisdom*, by John O'Donohue, © HarperCollins Publishers Inc., 1998, p. 128. Used by permission.

Accepting one another does not mean being resigned to one's own and to others' "awkward, disturbing and negative presences." It does mean that participants accept these so that they may develop authentically. Beginning to engage in intentional spiritual disciplines will certainly not make anyone automatically a flawless person. Rather, as participants find new ways to be honest with themselves, certain "awkward, disturbing, and negative presences" which they may have hidden or ignored in the past will sometimes emerge quite unexpectedly. Participants need to accept others and themselves openly and graciously otherwise they will be very disappointed and unduly judgmental when they come upon some aspect of themselves or others that they do not like.

Challenging

When you are faithful to the risk and ambivalence of growth, you are engaging your life. The soul loves risk; it is only through the door of risk that growth can enter.

John O'Donohue[11]

> Encouraging the value of challenge within small groups encourages honesty within the groups and helps participants to be open to know themselves and others more fully. Challenge promotes personal and group authenticity and compassion for others.

Without challenge there is no personal or community growth. Responding to challenge in a caring and creative way involves taking the risk to see things for what they are. Sometimes we may resist opening ourselves to challenges to who we are or what we think. We may not want to admit to what we see. This can lead to internal personal conflict that will affect the way that we participate within the group, for example, by becoming defensive or overly guarded in what we say.

We also may not want to admit to what others see in us. We may feel that we are under attack by their challenges. This can also lead to defensiveness and possibly to conflict with other participants.

---

[11] *Anam Cara: A Book of Celtic Wisdom*, by John O'Donohue © HarperCollins Publishers Inc., 1998, p. 128. Used by permission.

Conflict arising from challenge is not to be avoided, however. Differing views need to be voiced so that through honest discussion participants learn to honour their own and others' experiences. Parker Palmer warns congregations against projecting too much of a "nice family" image onto members. He writes, "When an idealized image of family is imposed upon the church, our experience in the congregation becomes constricted. Now the church—where we might experience creative conflict, heterogeneity and freedom for innovation—becomes dominated by the expectation of closeness and warmth."[12]

The group does not take it upon itself to expose and to get rid of the participants' delinquent qualities as discussed above. Rather, accepting their own and each other's short-comings is a significant first step to the honesty and compassionate truth-telling necessary for healing and growth.

Marsha Sinetar observes that "it is usually not conflict or disappointment that causes problems, but our way of handling them." Conflict is handled more kindly in an atmosphere of affirmation and acceptance. As Sinetar goes on to say, "the wider our affinity for someone, the easier it is to resolve seeming conflicts."[13]

Challenge can help the group avoid becoming too self-centered or short-sighted, resisting new ideas. All groups need to be willing to challenge themselves so that they remain open to the movement of the Spirit and to new possibilities for growth and ministry.

Celebratory

Celebration reminds us who we are; in this case, fellow travellers discovering the blessings and challenges of life in community with God and with others.

Being part of a small group ministry includes prayerful acceptance and challenge. It should also be fun! Groups are encouraged to find ways to celebrate their time together. Each meeting, can be seen as a celebration of gathering, doing something of interest together, and growing spiritually.

---

[12] Parker Palmer, *Company of Strangers: Christians and the Renewal of America's Public Life*, (New York: Crossroad, 1983), p. 134. Used by permission.

[13] Marsha Sinetar, *The Mentor's Spirit: Life Lessons on Leadership and the Art of Encouragement*, (New York: St. Martin's Press, 1998), p. 141. Used by permission.

In small groups, celebration affirms the joy of being together, through good times and challenging times. Celebration also accentuates the gifts participants share with the group and the groups' gifts, shared with the congregation.

Safe

As a safe group develops, it becomes easier for the group to carry out its ministry. In other words, the group becomes increasingly open to the Spirit moving in and through the group, and more able to respond.

Safe groups help participants take part freely. Within safe groups participants know they are respected and that confidentiality will be honoured. This is especially important for those who are new to the church. For those who are uncertain of their faith and spirituality, or have had unpleasant experiences with a church in the past, or are concerned about participating in a group for any reason, the safety of a group is critical.

Creating a safe space means helping participants feel that they can be as open as they choose to be, while at the same time knowing that openness always poses risks. Participants can never be certain how their journey together may unfold. The group cannot be safe if that means protecting everyone from things they do not want to feel or hear. Through the small group process, the development of a covenant, the recognition of core values, and with skilled facilitation, participants can take risks as safely as possible while recognizing that every journey to know oneself, others, and the Divine more deeply takes unexpected turns. Creating a safe space means that fear is honoured and held in trust.

Part II
Putting Small Group Ministry into Practice

Chapter 5
Getting Started

This chapter discusses one approach to help a congregation consider small group ministry as a way of nurturing faith in its congregational life.

There are a few basic principles behind this approach:

❖ Congregations learn how to do small group ministry by doing it.

❖ Congregations need to maintain their focus on small group ministry as a way to nurture faith that leads to Spirit-led ministry.

❖ Congregations' ministries will differ depending on their contexts and circumstances.

❖ There is no fail-safe, step-by-step plan to develop small group ministry. Congregations, or groups within the congregation, may make mistakes as they develop small group ministry. This is not to be seen as something negative but part of what learning and growing is all about.

❖ Good facilitation, whether there is one group in the congregation or 20, is key to the development of small group ministry.

❖ Congregations are encouraged to have a small group ministry coordinating team.

Starting a Covenant Group

The first step of considering small group ministry is for one or two groups to develop a covenant (see Chapter 8) to explore small group ministry for six weeks. It is advisable that a ministry personnel person is part of each group. These groups follow the small group meeting format: Opening, Check-in, Spiritual Practice, Group Interest, Check-out, and Closing (see Chapter 7). They use the group interest time of the meeting to explore what small group ministry is all about. A suggested scripture passage to use for the spiritual practice, "Praying with Scripture," is provided for each meeting.

The group interest time of the meeting might look like the following:

Week One: Introduction (Matt. 14:13–21)
Participants share experiences of being in groups, considering questions such as:

❖ What assumptions do we bring about participating in groups?

❖ What have been some of our good experiences? Some unfavourable experiences?

❖ How have groups helped me to nurture my faith?

Week Two: What is Small Group Ministry All About? (Matt. 15:21–28)
(Group develops its covenant.)
Before meeting, participants read the introduction and Chapters 1 and 2 of *Rooted in the Divine* and discuss these. Participants also read Chapter 8, The Group Covenant, to prepare to develop a covenant.

Week Three: What is Small Group Ministry All About? (Mark 4:15–41)
Continue the discussion from the previous meeting. Participants read Chapters 3 and 4 of *Rooted in the Divine* before the meeting and discuss these together.

Week Four: Groups in our Congregation (Mark 7:31–37)
Participants consider such questions as:

❖ What is the history of groups in our congregation? When did they begin? Do the same people participate in many of the groups? Who leads? How are leaders trained? How is what happens in our groups reflected in other aspects of our congregational life and worship?

❖ How can we help the congregation understand the importance of spiritual growth and faith formation?

❖ How can we stress the importance of participants nurturing their faith through small groups while also recognizing that there are other ways for individuals to develop spiritually?

Week Five: Facilitating Small Group Ministry (Luke 2:41–51)
Participants read and discuss Chapter 9, Facilitating Small Groups, and consider the following questions:

❖ Who are the potential facilitators in our congregation?

❖ Would we like to become facilitators? Are we able to take on that role?

❖ How will facilitators be trained? What would that training look like?

Week Six: Bringing our Covenant to a Close (Luke 11:5–13)
Re-read Chapter 8, particularly the section on evaluation. Discuss some of the following questions, as appropriate for the group:

❖ What have we learned from being together?

❖ What have been the blessings of being together?

❖ Have there been any regrets?

❖ What might we do differently another time?

❖ Is there a biblical image that describes our experience together?

❖ What are our next steps? For example, develop a small group ministry co-ordinating team. (See below.)

❖ Do we want to educate the congregation about small group ministry?

❖ Might we consider providing facilitation for new groups?

❖ What approach might we take to create covenant groups?

❖ What elements of the small group process might we incorporate into some of the groups that already exist?

Bring the group covenant to a close. Celebrate.

The Congregational Small Group Ministry Coordinating Team

One way to help support and sustain small group ministry is to have a congregational small group ministry coordinating team. The role of the team (a covenant group of three or four participants) is to promote and support small group ministry in the congregation. The group considers ways to:

❖ Encourage new groups to form; it is not the team's role to approve groups

❖ Help to coordinate leadership development, perhaps including training new facilitators

❖ Receive and distribute information pertinent to small group ministry to group facilitators

❖ Provide the congregation with information about existing groups through the weekly bulletin, a small group ministry newsletter, bulletin board, or Web site

❖ Encourage groups to share learnings from their ministry experiences

❖ Provide support for small group ministry facilitators including encouraging, and perhaps facilitating, a group or groups for small group facilitators

❖ Find ways to celebrate the diversity of ministry within the congregation

The minister might facilitate the small group ministry coordinating team until there is someone in the congregation who wishes or is available to do so. Some congregations may wish to hire a staff associate to take on this role.

The facilitator of the coordinating team should be familiar with spiritual nurture through small group ministry, and should also be engaged in, and willing to teach, spiritual practices. The facilitator should also have experience in small group facilitation.

The team may wish to have a workshop on small group ministry to explain what it is all about and see what kinds of groups people might like to form.

A couple of guiding questions to help the congregation think about possible small groups are:

❖ Where do you experience God in your life?

❖ What experiences or activities bring you closer to God?

❖ What is life giving for you?

Some possible answers are:

❖ Praying, meditating

❖ Gardening

❖ Singing

❖ Walking in the woods, the country, the mountains, by the sea, or in the city

❖ Gathering for coffee or tea with friends

❖ Having fun with my friends – e.g. playing cards, hockey, tennis

❖ Drawing, painting, sculpting

❖ Writing poetry, short stories

❖ Walking the labyrinth

❖ Canoeing or kayaking

❖ Cycling

❖ Cooking

❖ Knitting, crocheting, sewing, quilting

❖ Bird watching

❖ Reading the Bible

❖ Reading poetry, novels, or short stories

❖ Studying books that raise religious and theological questions

❖ Watching the stars

❖ Listening to music

❖ Visiting the sick

❖ Working with the Out of the Cold program

❖ Teaching Sunday school

❖ Helping to plan worship

❖ Developing rituals to express my growing faith

❖ Being involved in governance groups: boards, sessions, etc.

The next question to ask the congregation would be:

❖ Would anyone like to get together with others and start a small group related to any of these activities?

Those who are already involved in groups may wish to restructure their group as an intentional small group ministry, develop a covenant, and follow the small group format.

The team could offer some initial leadership training in developing a covenant and spiritual practices for interested facilitators. Training for spiritual practices could begin with teaching Praying with Scripture. (See page 66.)

Chapter 6
The Meeting Space

The nature of the group and availability of space will dictate where the group meets. Groups need to consider if they need a quiet space or one that will offer them some privacy.

For many groups it is best to have participants sit in a circle. Sometimes sitting around a table is the most comfortable way to meet, lounging around in easy chairs works best for others. It is important that all participants are able to see and hear each other. The group needs to be mindful of anyone who is hearing impaired or has another condition that makes it more difficult for them to participate in a group and be sure that her or his needs are meet.

Creating a Worship Centre

It is also advisable that each group creates a worship centre – especially for the opening, check-in, checkout, and closing. If having the group meet in a circle around a worship centre isn't suitable for the group interest time, consider having two different areas for the meeting.

A worship centre provides focus for the group and the symbols of its life together. It is a place for simple rituals and creative expression.

The worship centre does not have to be elaborate— it can be as simple as a small table and a candle. It is, however, an opportunity for creatively exploring symbols, images, and creating "spiritual art."

To help make the worship centre meaningful for the group, consider the following options:

❖ Participants might take turns bringing in objects to create a different centre for each meeting.

❖ During the spiritual practices segment of the meeting, participants could create objects that could be used for the worship centre, such as mandalas, prayer candles, clay images, or drawings.

❖ Participants could each bring in something new to add, perhaps following a different theme each time, so that the centre develops over the course of the group's life.

Adapt the chart on the next page to help plan your meeting space and worship centre.

Meeting Date	Room set-up: Who's doing it? What's needed?	Worship Centre: Who's doing it? What's needed?	Any other issues to consider?

Chapter 7
The Small Group Meeting

Each of us needs the community of faith to help find clues for faithfulness in an often bewildering world.[14]

Parker Palmer

The small group meeting consists of the following meeting format:

1. Meal (optional)
2. Gathering Time
3. Opening
4. Check-in
5. Spiritual Practices/Prayer
6. Group Interest
7. Check-out
8. Closing

Each element has a specific purpose to help create community, nurture faith, and help participants enjoy their time together as fully as possible. Groups differ depending on their needs and interests. The format therefore may be adjusted to suit the group's particular situation.

This format is based on a small group meeting for 2-2½ hours, in addition to having a meal together. Individual groups will adjust times to suit their own needs.

Meal (optional)
(Suggested time: ½ - 2 hours)

> *Isn't a meal together the most beautiful expression of our desire to be given to each other in our brokenness? The table, the food, the drinks, the words, the stories: are they not the most intimate ways in which we not only express the desire to give ourselves to each other, but also do this in actuality?*

Henri Nouwen[15]

---

[14] Parker Palmer, *Company of Strangers: Christians and the Renewal of America's Public Life*, (New York: Crossroad, 1983), p. 162. Used by permission.

[15] Henri Nouwen, *The Life of the Beloved: Spiritual Living in a Secular World*, (New York: Crossroad/Herder & Herder, 2002), p. 88. Used by permission.

Groups are encouraged to begin their meeting with a meal, to break bread together. Some groups may decide to have a meal at each meeting. Some may decide to have a meal at their first and last meetings. Once participants decide if they are going to have a meal and how often, they need to decide how to organize it. For example:

❖ order in pizza, chicken, or Chinese, Japanese, Vietnamese food, etc.

❖ buy a ready-made meal from the supermarket

❖ go potluck

❖ one or two people could prepare a meal each time for the group

❖ a variation of the above to suit the group's needs (are there allergies to consider?) and resources (time and money)

Participants also need to decide how long they wish to spend sharing a meal together (groups will probably need at least an hour to have a relaxed time together), and which parts of the meeting they might incorporate into the meal.

Gathering

(Suggested time: 15 - 20 min. prior to meeting)

Groups that do not have a meal together are encouraged to allow approximately 15-20 minutes prior to the scheduled meeting time for participants to gather.

The gathering time provides an opportunity for participants to socialize before the meeting begins. This helps to promote community building, allowing participants to get to know each other better. It also helps participants focus on the purpose of the meeting by providing a transition between the events of the day and the small group meeting.

The group may wish to serve refreshments at this time. If so, participants will have to decide who will take on that responsibility.

Some groups may incorporate new members into the group once the covenant period begins. The facilitator can meet with newcomers before the meeting begins, and newcomers can meet other participants as the group gathers together. In addition, anyone who has missed a meeting can be brought up to date during the gathering.

Note: Care should always be taken that the gathering time does not extend beyond the time the meeting is scheduled to begin. The meeting should start on time.

The Opening

(Suggested time: 5 min.)

The purpose of the opening is to recognize that the participants are coming together as a group for an agreed-upon purpose. The opening helps participants call attention to God's presence, prepare to explore their spirituality, deepen their prayer life, and take part in the group's activity.

The facilitator may do the opening, or the group may decide that participants will take turns.

The facilitator calls participants together by dimming the lights, playing some music, or ringing a bell. If the group has a worship centre (see Chapter 6), it will gather there for the opening.

The opening may include

❖ a prayer

❖ a ritual act such as lighting a candle to symbolize God's presence

❖ a poem or a song

(For some suggestions, see Openings, Appendix 1)

If the small group meeting begins with a meal, its opening may form the grace for the meal, which could include prayer and song.

Alternatively, once the meal is over, an opening can act as a transition between the meal and the rest of the meeting.

Check-in

(Suggested time 15 - 20 min.)

The check-in is a time for each participant to share personally. This is an extremely important part of the meeting. The check-in provides the opportunity for community building so that trust can develop and participants can feel more at ease about exploring their spirituality within the context of their particular small group focus.

For the check-in, the facilitator invites each participant to reflect upon a question. The question could be as simple as, How are you this evening? Or a more specific question could be used such as, Where have you experienced God in your life since we last met? The second question is effective for it helps participants to begin to be aware of the way that God is active in their lives, an activity which is at the very basis of spiritual development. There are also many other approaches that can be used (see Check-ins, Appendix 1).

It should be made clear to all participants that this is a time to listen rather than a discussion time. Since small group ministry encourages spiritual nurture, it is important that participants find ways to listen to each other so that growth can take place. It is also a time to begin intentional listening for God as participants listen to each other. "Cross talk," therefore, should be avoided. Each participant talks without comment from the rest of the participants. If it seems appropriate, a clarifying question may be asked. There should not be any judgmental comments—good or bad—so as to avoid what might be called "check-in competition" and "check-in anxiety."

The group may wish to use a talking stick, talking stone, or other object, which may be passed around the circle, or placed on a table and picked up by whoever wishes to speak. Only the person with the object speaks. Many groups find such a practice helps everyone to listen and avoid discussion, as those who tend rarely to speak are assured of their time, and those who tend to speak often are encouraged to use their time well. Participants should feel free to disclose as little or as much as they wish, and should always have the option to pass.

If the group begins its meeting with a meal, consider having the check-in at the beginning of the meal. If the check-in process feels too rigid for a meal, it can be done after the meal, during the formal part of the meeting.

Keep in mind that a lot of talking during the meal does not necessarily mean that people have checked-in. The check-in allows for participants to "listen" intentionally to each other and to begin focusing on the movements of the spirit in their own lives and within the group.

For at least the first couple of meetings it is advisable that the facilitator goes first. After checking-in the facilitator might then ask if someone else in the group would like to speak until everyone has checked-in, or the facilitator might suggest participants go one by one around the circle.

Both models are useful. The first allows the participants to speak when they are ready. Participants who are less confident with the process or need time to gather their thoughts do not feel put on the spot. The second model tends to go more quickly, but it also means that participants have to respond in turn. Although participants have to speak in turn, it provides the opportunity for everyone to practice this skill.

The check-in is supposed to be fairly brief. If there is someone who just likes to talk, the facilitator needs gently to remind her or him of the need to keep the check-in short.

Occasionally, someone may be experiencing some sort of personal difficulty and may need to speak about it at some length. Depending on the situation, it may be appropriate to offer the necessary pastoral care to that person at that time. If someone has a serious concern, the group is encouraged to take time to pray for that person.

Sometimes check-ins may take over the meeting. For example, if someone raises an issue that the group feels it should discuss, or if something comes up that suggests a change in agenda, the group may wish to make a change. The facilitator should, however, be sure that everyone agrees. It is also a good idea to complete the initial check-in and then come back to whatever has arisen.

Some participants who are anxious to get on with the content of the meeting may resist check-in, suggesting that it is a waste of time. The facilitator should encourage the check-in, stressing its importance both as a community-building tool to help develop trust within the group, and also as a good opportunity for participants to develop their listening skills. For what may seem to be "more formal" meetings, such as a group that meets around finances and wishes to develop the group as small group ministry, experience proves that meetings that have a check-in time at the beginning run more smoothly.

Spiritual Practices/Prayer

(Suggested time: 20 - 30 min.)

Prayer during the meeting is important: it helps participants discover and explore spiritual practices that they can use together, and individually. In addition, as the group develops as an intentional community of faith, it will become aware of the movement of the Spirit in its midst, and will learn how to respond in faith.

Participants are encouraged to develop their prayer life together by exploring various kinds of prayer and practising some of them together. Depending on the nature of the prayer or spiritual practice, the time needed may vary from week to week. Some groups may choose to explore a different form of prayer each week. Others may prefer to follow a particular type of prayer or a spiritual practice at each meeting. (For a discussion of some types of group prayer and spiritual practices, see Chapter 11.)

As with the check-in, the facilitator will probably lead the prayer time. However, there may be several people who are comfortable leading prayer and who wish to take turns.

One form of group prayer that is easy to lead and very effective in small groups is "Praying with Scripture," also known as the African Bible Reflection, or the Lambeth method. (See page 66 for details.)

Group Interest

(Suggested time: 1 hour)

This portion of the meeting is devoted to the interest that brought the group together in the first place. This will, therefore, vary from group to group. (See Chapter 10.)

Using Resource People

Sometimes the facilitator may lead the opening, check-in, prayer, check-out, and closing, and a resource person may lead the group interest segment. This may often be the case with groups that form to learn about a social justice issue such as globalization or literacy, or with groups interested in developing new skills such as story-telling, cooking, or financial planning.

Many groups find it most helpful when the resource person agrees to facilitate this part of the small group meeting for, say, six weeks, and is also willing to participate in the rest of the meeting, and to accept the terms of the group covenant with all participants.

One Small Group Example

Eight people in a congregation get together every Thursday evening to play euchre. They have been meeting for two years, covenanting for eight weeks at a time. They follow the small group process as presented above. Every week the participants pray with the scriptures as their form of spiritual practice.

One week the facilitator of the worship team comes to the group and asks if the participants would be willing to share some of their experience with the rest of the congregation during a Sunday service. The group agrees. Three weeks later the group sets up two card tables at the front of the sanctuary and during the sermon time the participants talk about what the group has meant for them.

❖ One participant says that his own contemplative nature has been affirmed by the group, and he is able to tap into his inner sense of peace more and more in his stressful work situation.

❖ Another says she appreciates the fun and the laughter that they have together, as she tends to take life very seriously. She adds that she has also learned some good euchre strategies.

❖ A third participant, who is going through a divorce, talks about the personal support she has received from the rest of the group

❖ Another says that he is profoundly moved every week as the group prays for each other. His sense of connection to the rest of the group through prayer is a profound gift for him.

The group has decided that they feel called to speak with the facilitator of the Out of the Cold group to see if they can come in once a month and offer to play cards with the women and men who attend the program. If it seems appropriate, in the future they will also see if there is any interest on the part of the Out of the Cold participants to join with them in the spiritual exercise of Praying with Scripture.

Check-out

(Suggested time: 10 - 15 min.)

The check-out is a brief time for each participant to reflect on the meeting and share that reflection with the rest of the group. If the group has a worship centre (see Chapter 6), they will gather there for the check-out and closing.

The check-out is important for the individuals in the group and for the group as a whole. It helps the participants to bring some of their thoughts and feelings together as the meeting is coming to a close.

The check-out also encourages the participants to be aware of each other. Is someone upset? Is someone angry? Is there a group issue that needs to be attended to before the meeting ends? Is there an issue between any of the participants that they need to attend to?

As with the check-in, each participant speaks without any cross-talk or judgmental comments.

The facilitator may want to find a way to focus the check-out question to help participants bring their thoughts together. Questions related to spiritual nurture could be: What has been a blessing for you this evening? Where have you sensed God's presence during our time together?

As another option, participants may be asked to think of a word, or an image arising from the meeting that is meaningful to them. This could be shared as part of the check-out, used as part of the participants' ongoing reflections between meetings, or both.

As part of the check-out, the group could have someone keep a "spiritual journal." Whoever keeps the journal would take a moment in prayerful silence and then reflect on where she or he felt the movement of the Spirit. Since this is practice may not be familiar to many, some participants may feel uncertain about doing this at first. The facilitator should encourage participants to write down whatever comes to them without feeling that they need to say the "right" thing. A different person might keep the journal at each meeting, passing it to another member at the end of the meeting.

(See Check-outs, Appendix 1.)

Closing

(Suggested time: 5 min.)

The closing symbolically brings the meeting to an end. As with the opening, the closing can be done in a number of ways. Each group will find a format with which it is most comfortable. The closing should be brief and may include a prayer followed or preceded by a ritual, poem, or a song (see Closings, Appendix 1).

The following chart, "Preparing for a Meeting," may be helpful for groups to use as they begin to think about meeting together. Feel free to photocopy the chart or adapt it for your own use.

Preparing for a Meeting

Part of Meeting	How might we do it?	What's needed?	Things to consider
Meal (optional)			
Gathering			
Opening			
Check-in			
Prayer/ Spiritual Practice			
Group Interest			
Check-out			
Closing			

Chapter 8
The Group Covenant

A covenant is an agreement, a contract, a promise, or a pledge. Within the Judeo-Christian tradition a covenant is an agreement between God and God's people.

Establishing a small group ministry covenant provides the opportunity for participants to develop guidelines for the group's time together. The covenant also reminds the participants that as they set out the group's norms or terms of agreement that the task upon which they are embarking is a holy task formed within community that is grounded in the divine.

Developing a Covenant

When people feel free to make a covenant for shorter time periods and also have the opportunity to agree to continue if they choose, they take personal responsibility for their participation within the congregation. This way, no one needs to be anxious about whether they, or others, should participate more, or differently, in the life of the faith community.

At the first meeting a blank copy of the group covenant is given to everyone (see the sample on page 51). At the second meeting, the group takes time to fill it in and be sure that everyone understands it and is in agreement.

While many of these details (such as meeting time and place) have to be worked out before the group first gathers, having the group review these details and agree to them formally gives the opportunity to change some of them early on in the group's life. Everyone will also understand the purpose of the group and what is expected of them, and will have an enhanced sense of belonging to the group. While the facilitator helps to make sure the group runs smoothly, the group needs to be able to make decisions together.

Once the covenant has been agreed upon, the group can carry out a small ritual—for example, a prayer and a song—to acknowledge it. The group may want to have a symbol of the covenant that is part of the worship centre. All the participants should have a copy of the covenant. This is a group "possession."

As the group meets, if something to which it has covenanted is not working, the group should revisit the covenant and see about the possibility of changing it. For example, if a group agrees to meet for two hours but finds it really needs to meet for two hours to do everything it needs to do, they might consider changing the covenant. The group needs to be serious about their covenant but not so rigid that it hinders the group in any way.

If changes are made to the covenant, it is very important that all of the group's participants are given a copy of the changes.

The Purpose of the Group

The small group could be, for example, a scripture study group, a discussion group, a cooking group, a prayer group, or a governance group. One reason groups fail is that there is not a clear understanding amongst the participants as to why they are meeting. It is, therefore, very important that the nature of the group be clearly stated. If at some point the purpose of the group seems to be shifting, the group should to revisit its covenant and consider whether they need to revise it.

The Size of the Group

Six to eight is a good number of participants for most groups. A group with as few as three participants can also work well in some cases. Groups with more than nine or ten participants need to consider dividing.

New Members

Since community building is an important part of the small group work, the group needs to consider what would be a reasonable cut off date or if it is willing to try to incorporate new members into the group as the session progresses. This is not to be seen as being exclusive, but merely recognizing the importance of community building and the need for participants to be committed to be part of all the designated meetings. If someone is very interested in joining a group, she or he may have to wait until the next covenant period begins. Many groups, however, have success in bringing in new participants throughout the covenant period.

Covenant Length

Depending on the nature of the group it could agree to meet for four weeks, six weeks, or perhaps for as long as six months. Prayer groups, for example, may want to covenant for three to four months. It is important, however, that the group brings the covenant to an end and evaluates the meetings before beginning a new covenant period, even if the same participants are going to continue.

Having a designated session length also means that new people can come on board and former participants can leave graciously. Not everyone wants or is able to be tied into a group for an extended period of time. It is important, however, that barring unforeseen circumstances, participants honour their commitment to the group for the covenant period.

Meeting Frequency

How often the group meets will depend on the nature of the group and the schedules of those involved. Groups may meet weekly, monthly, or bi-weekly.

Meeting Length

The length of each session will also be determined by the nature of the group and participants' schedules. Two hours tends to be a good length for most meetings, which allows for one hour for the group interest section and another hour for the rest of the meeting. A "meal meeting" will be longer. Circumstances will determine what works best for each group.

Where Meetings are Held

Meetings may be held at the church, at someone's home or elsewhere, according to the group's needs, and availability of space.

The Facilitation Model

Possible facilitation models include: one facilitator, shared facilitation (two people take on the task together), rotating facilitation (a different person for each meeting).

Group Values

It is important that the participants name some of the core values that they see as important to carry out effective small group work. Groups need to consider what values participants bring to the group and what values they want to nurture and uphold within the group so that a healthy environment can be developed. The group may want to consider the PACCS approach to help them develop their core values. (See Chapter 4.)

Group Norms

As well as group values, each group needs to consider meeting norms that all members follow. These might include, for example, being present in mind, body, and spirit; beginning and ending on time; keeping to the meeting format; welcoming all questions; one person speaks while all others listen respectfully, and asking permission of each other before offering feedback.

Confidentiality

Small group work usually involves a lot of personal story-telling. As the group develops, the degree of personal disclosure may also develop. It is very important, therefore, that the group addresses issues of confidentiality. The group may decide to adopt, for example, a policy of complete confidentiality, which means that nothing that is said within the group goes beyond the group. While in principle this is desirable, this is difficult to carry out. Even when there is a high degree of respect for others, people often share their experiences with friends and family.

The group may prefer to adopt a policy of discretionary confidentiality. In this case the group agrees that stories can be shared but that names won't be used. While this allows participants to share stories outside the group and therefore can help the participants process more fully what is happening within the group, "story-telling" is certainly not desirable when it is done to entertain others. Participants can lose sight of crossing lines of confidentiality when they simply enjoy telling the next episode of their small group meeting experience. Where there is discretionary confidentiality, participants may also ask that certain personal stories do not go beyond the group.

Bringing the Covenant to an End

Bringing a small group covenant to an end provides the opportunity for group reflection, sharing gratitude and regrets, and evaluation. The group can celebrate its life and ministry together. Participants may leave the group if they need or wish to, and another group may start, with new participants.

Group Evaluation

The last meeting of any covenant period should be dedicated to closure. The general interest time of this meeting, therefore, is used for reflection, evaluation, and celebration.

Evaluation is vital to the success of small group ministry. As a way to help participants evaluate the small group experience, consider asking some of the following questions:

❖ What are your feelings right now?

❖ Is it difficult for you to bring this commitment to an end? If so, can you explain why?

❖ In there any unfinished business that needs to be attended to?

❖ Has your understanding of ministry changed from this group experience? If so, how?

❖ What image or symbol might you use to describe your relationship to the group experience?

❖ What biblical stories or themes describe your experience with the group?

❖ Do other experiences of endings or saying good-bye come to mind?

❖ For what do you feel gratitude from the group as a whole and from each participant in the group?

❖ For what do you feel regret during the covenant period?

❖ What symbol, word, or image would you like to give to others to remember this experience together?

❖ What has worked? What might be changed?

❖ How have we fulfilled our ministry to the group's participants, to the congregation, and to the wider community?

Some groups may want to continue to meet. After completing its evaluation and bringing the commitment to an end, the group should consider any changes that it might make to a new covenant. Participants may also decide that they want to form a new interest group that reflects a new direction in their understanding of ministry.

A short ritual recognizing that the group's covenant time is over is very helpful to the participants. Celebrate your time together.

Small Group Ministry Covenant

The members of _____

at _____

agree to meet every _____

from _____ to _____

at _____ .

We will meet for a _____ covenant period

beginning _____ and ending _____ .

We agree that we will _____ or will _____ not accept new members

into the group after we begin our covenant period.

The purpose of our group is _____

_____

Group facilitation will be provided by _____

_____

The norms and values that the group wishes to uphold are:

1. _____

2. _____

3. _____

4. _____

5. _____

Concerning issues of confidentiality, we agree that _____

_____

We agree that at the end of the covenant period we will bring closure to the group, and evaluate the session before considering whether we will re-establish the group and develop a new covenant.

Names of participants:

_____

_____

_____

_____

_____

Chapter 9
Facilitating Small Groups

To facilitate a group is to respond to God's call to use one's spiritual and inter-personal gifts in the context of an interest or passion that one shares with others. It is to be in community with others who have a common interest, and to assist them to develop community so that, through that common interest, faith can be deepened.

God draws us into community to work with God and with others. A facilitator has a specific role to play within a group, supporting everyone to further develop trust in God, and to live out that trust in community. The facilitator, however, supports a group to do the work it has chosen to do, rather than directs or controls the group. Facilitation has more to do with following a group than deciding where it goes, or what it does.

Characteristics of Small Group Ministry Facilitators

No matter what other skills, training or gifts individuals may have, the way that they facilitate a small group ministry group will reflect their faith and spirituality.

Being grounded in their own faith is the primary characteristic of small group ministry facilitators. Other characteristics will affect the facilitators' faith formation. This is a two-way process. Facilitation skills develop as facilitators nurture their faith and the facilitators' faith and spirituality will deepen as they develop their facilitation skills.

Finding facilitators who are intentionally developing their own faith life is very important. There is a wisdom that comes with spiritual growth. Facilitators need to be comfortable talking about spiritual growth so that they can encourage others to be comfortable as well.

At the heart of spiritual development is a growing humility. One of the root meaning of humility is "humus," or earth. To be humble has to do with being rooted in the ground of our being, the Divine, and not in arrogant pride. Humility is a strength that is born of God's love for oneself and experiencing that deep gracious love for others. Humility has to do with seeing things for what they are and being open to the reality of God's presence, that is to say, God's love for and in everyone. Love for others is grounded in compassion and generosity.

Facilitators are not necessarily further along the spiritual path than the rest of the group. They are travelling with them. The group meets to journey together. The facilitator is there to help facilitate the journey.

Here are some small group ministry goals and some characteristics facilitators would need to help groups reach those goals.

Small Group Ministry Goals *Small Groups:*	**Leadership Characteristic** *Facilitators:*
1. nurture faith	1. are actively developing their own faith and spirituality through some form of prayer life or spiritual discipline
2. build a community that is both affirming and challenging	2. have good group building skills; can create a trusting environment; can set clear boundaries for themselves and others; and do not shy away from conflict
3. empower participants	3. are compassionate and open to others; are good listeners; and encourage integrity in themselves and others
4. encourage members to nurture their faith while joining others with a common interest or passion	4. have a particular interest or passion and recognize the relationship between that interest and spiritual growth
5. develop and carry out a group covenant	5. help the group develop and fulfill its covenant
6. explore and develop the group's ministry goals	6. help the group develop its ministry goals
7. help to create an atmosphere in which participants can have a "good time"	7. enjoy being with people; have a sense of humour, a sense of beauty beauty, and a zeal for life

Ministry Personnel as Small Group Leaders

It is probably not feasible for the congregation's ministry personnel to facilitate all the small groups. Even if it were, it would not be advisable. Ministry personnel must be willing to encourage the spiritual growth of others so that they can take on leadership roles. This is certainly not to say that ministry personnel should never lead a small group. It may be appropriate for ministry personnel to do so. She or he, however, needs to intentionally encourage the development of lay leadership for small groups.

Ministry personnel can:

❖ encourage the development of a small group ministry co-ordinating team;

❖ identify potential facilitators;

❖ provide initial and ongoing training for the facilitators or find ways for others to train facilitators;

❖ encourage facilitators to begin groups, including a small group for facilitators to share their experiences and to learn from each other;

❖ model aspects of the small group process in meetings that they lead, such as check-ins and check-outs, prayer, and having someone keep a spiritual journal.

Training Facilitators for Small Group Ministry

There are three key areas in which a facilitator needs training:

❖ Personal spiritual nurture: various forms of prayer and spiritual disciplines to nurture the facilitator

❖ Group spiritual nuture: various forms of prayer and spiritual disciplines to nurture groups

❖ Community building skills: small group process and group dynamics

The congregation may have ministry personnel or people affiliated with the congregation who have some experience in facilitation. These people may be willing to begin a group that focuses on their area of expertise. For example, someone may be able to start a small group on spiritual nurture and teach different forms of prayer. Someone else may be able to start a group on the basics of group dynamics. Someone may have some experience with the process of spiritual discernment and want to facilitate a group that focuses on that area. These groups would follow the small group format and in effect be a part of the congregation's small group ministry.

Training in spiritual nurture and practice, and group dynamics, is provided for congregations by United Church education centres: Naramata, in British Columbia; Prairie Christian Training Centre in Saskatchewan; Stewart House and Five Oaks in Ontario; and Tatamagouche in Nova Scotia.

Personnel at the General Council Office and at the Conference offices can also provide training for congregations. Workshops could be developed for individual congregations or for clusters of congregations. Congregations can also seek out training programs offered by other denominations.

Those congregations that have no one trained in spiritual practices or small group dynamics and for whatever reason find it difficult to connect with the education centres, Conference or General Council staff, need to begin with what they've got. If there are people in the congregation who are interested in developing small group ministry, they can learn by doing. They can seek out books on spiritual nurture, and community building, form a small group covenant, and explore these subjects and what they mean for themselves as facilitators and for their congregation. After they complete their covenant time together, they can apply what they are learning to a group they wish to lead. Through leading a group they will begin to train others as they also learn the small group process and spiritual disciplines.

Chapter 10
Examples of Small Groups

Congregations can have many different types of small groups. The possibilities are endless. Congregational small groups must arise out of the interests and passions of those in the congregation. A few people can start a group, but those individuals should be sincerely interested in taking part.

This chapter outlines examples of small groups and considerations to keep in mind in terms of:

❖ **Purpose:** what distinguishes this from other small groups

❖ **Format:** anything about the general meeting format that these groups need to consider in particular

❖ **Facilitation:** particular leadership concerns that need to be considered

❖ **Possible Challenges:** while all groups face many challenges, highlighted here are one or two possible issues that may arise that are particularly related to this type of group

Prayer Groups

Purpose: To learn and practice various forms of prayer and other spiritual disciplines
Format: These groups follow the small group ministry meeting format except that the prayer/spiritual discipline time and the group interest time are combined.
Facilitation: The facilitator should be comfortable leading prayer. The facilitator may or may not have a lot of experience with prayer and spiritual disciplines but should be eager to learn and wish for others to learn as well.
Possible Challenges: Be mindful of the various ministry aspects of the group, and link the group's activity to the congregation and to the wider world.

Study Groups

Purpose: To study a book or several articles of interest.
Format: Study groups need to be clear about how they are approaching the study material such as how many chapters are to be studied at each meeting. It is important that all participants are aware of the schedule so that everyone is "on the same page," so to speak. At the beginning of each meeting, check which chapters everyone has read.

Facilitation: The facilitator needs to keep a gentle sense of humour if participants are not able to either keep up with reading or read the wrong chapter—it does happen. Encourage participants to come and participate as best they can, even if they haven't read the material, rather than not come at all.

Possible Challenges: Groups often study theological books. Some groups may feel that they do not have anyone in the group with the theological training to be able to lead the discussion. The adage "begin with what you've got" goes a long way here. The facilitator may not know any more than the rest of the participants but the group can work through the material together based on the participants' knowledge and experience.

The group may also know of someone in the community who does know a lot about the material and invite that person to facilitate the discussion time. The group may or may not pay the facilitator an honorarium to do this. It is important, however, that the guest facilitator be a part of all the sessions as a participant and be willing to uphold the group covenant.

Participation in study groups tends to be intellectual. This is important and stimulating. Occasionally, participants may resist the prayer part of the meeting, as they want to get on with the discussion. Facilitators may find it helpful to note that discussion becomes an even richer experience when participants spend time in prayer before turning to the book. Group prayer helps the head and the heart to meet. Study groups need to be mindful of the various ministry aspects of the group, and link the group's activity to the congregation and to the wider community.

Scripture Study Groups

Purpose: To study scripture.

Format: Group activity time will focus on studying a passage or series of passages from the Bible. Groups will have to decide which biblical passages are to be prepared prior to meeting.

Facilitation: Some groups may feel that they do not have anyone in the group with the theological or biblical studies training to be able to lead a Bible study. As with other study groups the adage "begin with what you've got" also goes a long way here. The facilitator may not know any more than the rest of the participants but the group can work through the material together based on the participants' experience.

The minister may wish to begin such a small group. Whoever leads should participate fully as a covenanted member of the group.

Possible Challenges: Be mindful of the various ministry aspects of the group, and link the group's activity to the congregation and to the wider community.

Choirs

Purpose: To sing.
Format: These groups follow the small group ministry meeting format.
Facilitation: The choir leader may prefer to facilitate only the group activity time while one of the choir members facilitates the rest of the small group time.
Possible Challenges: Developing and carrying out a group covenant. Choir members might commit to meet for a number of months, bring the group covenant to a close and evaluate. Evaluation helps participants to consider ways to enrich their own group experience as well to share their relationship to the rest of the congregation. Choirs will often be larger than most small groups. They may need to break into small groups for check-in and spiritual practice.

Choirs also need to find ways to connect with other congregational groups so that their experiences and learnings can be reflected in the music the choir provides for the congregation.

Women's Groups

Purpose: Specifically for women, with any purpose, but often these are spirituality groups.
Format: These groups follow the small group ministry meeting format.
Leadership: The facilitator must be able to create a safe environment for women. Women's groups work well with shared leadership.
Possible Challenges: Links with the rest of the congregation need to be nurtured to avoid the group becoming isolated from the rest of the faith community.

Men's Groups

Purpose: Specifically for men, with any purpose, but often these are fellowship groups.
Format: These groups follow the small group ministry meeting format.
Leadership: Strong leadership is needed to create a safe environment for men to discuss their spirituality, and to help nurture spiritual growth in a non-competitive setting.
Possible Challenges: Addressing men's spiritual needs in concert with their needs for fellowship.

Outreach Groups

Purpose: To meet around a specific outreach task, such as the Out of the Cold program, a community need, or perhaps in response to the church's mission theme.
Format: The group interest time focuses on the outreach concern.
Facilitation: The facilitator may feel more comfortable with the group's interest than with leading prayer. In such a case, shared facilitation may be preferred.
Possible Challenges: To take time for both spiritual nurture as well as the task at hand.

Hospitality Groups

Purpose: To make the congregation a welcoming place for everyone.
Format: These groups follow the small group ministry meeting format. During the group activity time ways to make the congregation more welcoming are considered. Such related topics as the theology of hospitality could also be considered.
Facilitation: Could be lead by one person or the leadership could be shared.
Possible Challenges: To see the group as an important time for spiritual growth for its members. To consider ways for the congregation to be more hospitable to the Spirit of God.

Support Groups

Purpose: To provide a specific type of support for the participants, such as personal support or fellowship, parents with young children, grief support, support for the under- or unemployed, or support for the family and friends of those with some identified issue or concern.
Format: These groups follow the small group ministry meeting format.
Facilitation: These groups must be well-facilitated, creating a very safe environment so that participants feel free to speak.
Possible Challenges: Confidentiality must be respected. These groups are not meant to be therapy groups.

General Interest Groups

Purpose: To develop and share a common interest, such as a chess group, cycling group, hiking group, movie group, or quilting group—the list is endless.
Format: These groups follow the small group ministry meeting format. Some groups, however, may need to consider how to adjust the meeting format in some circumstances, such as meeting outdoors.
Facilitation: The facilitator may feel more comfortable with the group's interest than with leading prayer. In such a case, shared facilitation may be preferred.

Possible Challenges: To be mindful of the various ministry aspects of the group, finding ways to make links to the congregation and to the wider community.

Governance Groups

Purpose: To perform tasks related to the general structure of the congregation, such as boards, councils, sessions, finance committees, worship committees, and ministry personnel committees.

Format: These groups follow the small group ministry meeting format. Group activity time is when the group's "business" is carried out.

Facilitation: One person may facilitate, or the responsibility may be shared meeting to meeting.

Possible Challenges: To carry out the prayer part of the meeting, and to be mindful of the various ministry aspects of the group.

All Groups

Some issues apply to all groups:

Purpose: Groups need to be clear about the interest that brought the participants together. If it seems to be changing during the covenant period, the group covenant needs to be reconsidered, and perhaps renegotiated.

Format: The small group meeting process needs to be followed so as to help build community and nurture spirituality without the process becoming a set of rules that end up hindering community building and spiritual nurture.

Facilitation: On the one hand, the facilitator needs to create an atmosphere that is not "controlled." On the other hand, the facilitator needs to follow through with her or his commitment to guide participants through the covenant period, and find ways to fulfill their ministry.

Possible Challenges: To be mindful of the various aspects of ministry, to the individual, the congregation and the wider community. To carry out a meaningful evaluation at the end of the covenant period. To avoid becoming "cliques" or "churches within the church."

Chapter 11
Prayer and Spiritual Discipline Groups

Rooted in the Divine stresses small group ministry as a way to nurture the participants' faith. This chapter describes three kinds of groups formed around prayer or spiritual disciplines: contemplative prayer, Praying with Scripture, and exploring prayer and spiritual practices.

Learning about and practicing prayer and spiritual disciplines is the purpose for each of these small groups. The times for prayer and for group activity are one unit. For these groups the meeting format is:

❖ meal

❖ gathering time

❖ opening

❖ check-in

❖ group interest – prayer/spiritual disciplines

❖ check-out

❖ closing

Contemplative or Centring Prayer Groups

There is an ancient tradition of "centring prayer" that is a traditional way of contemplation, sometimes described as "resting in God." Centring prayer develops a state of alert stillness in our minds and hearts as we consent to God's healing presence within us.

Through centring prayer we open ourselves up to God, to that light which can illuminate our beings. While centring prayer may appear to be a passive form of prayer, many people find that, as they are empowered by God's work within them, they can act with increased strength in daily life. The psalmist's words, "Be still and know that I am God," are a call into service, a call to live in the world out of a willingness to discern God's will.

In her book *Living Well*, author and Benedictine sister Joan Chittister writes, "Contemplation, the willingness to see as God sees, perhaps does not change the difficulty, the boredom, the evil of a pernicious, an insidious situation. But it can change the texture of our own hearts, the quality of our own responses, the depth of our own understandings."[16]

Trappist monk Thomas Keating has done extensive work on contemplative prayer. He views these as the seven fruits of centring prayer:

- You learn to discern what really matters—and let go instantly of what doesn't.
- You are less likely to judge other people.
- You accept your own basic goodness.
- You cultivate an open mind.
- Contemplative prayer deepens all types of prayer alone and in groups.
- You transform your motivations and purify your intentions.
- You achieve inner freedom to serve truthfully in the outer world.

Starting a Contemplative Prayer Group

Contemplative prayer groups work very well with three to seven participants. Once the group has formed it should develop a group covenant so that participants are aware of the nature of the group and of their commitment to the group (see Chapter 8).

Facilitating a Contemplative Prayer Group

While it is preferable that the facilitator has some experience in contemplative prayer, it is not necessary. The facilitator, however, must be comfortable leading prayer, and be able to create a safe environment to discuss prayer.

Preparation

Find a room that is quiet and where the prayer time won't be disturbed. Create an atmosphere appropriate for contemplative prayer. For example, arrange chairs in a circle, darken the room, and place a candle on a small table in the centre of the circle. Other objects that reflect the group's understanding of spirituality can be used to create a worship center. Provide pillows or cushions for anyone who may prefer to sit on the floor during the prayer time.

---

[16] From *Living Well*, by Joan D. Chittister. Copyright © 2000 by Joan D. Chittister. Published by Orbis Books, Maryknoll, New York 10545. Used by permission of the publisher.

Sample Contemplative Prayer Meeting

1. **Meal**

2. **Gathering**

3. **Lighting the candle**

   When the group is ready to begin, the facilitator asks a participant to light the candle on the worship table. The candle, which is a good centering device, symbolizes the presence of God who is always with us.

4. **Opening prayer**

   The opening prayer reflects the intention of coming together to open up to the power of the divine. It is preferable if the prayer is repeated slowly in unison. Facilitators can use prayers already written or write their own.

5. **Check-in**

   One effective check-in question might be, "Where have you experienced God in your life this week?" Discerning where participants see God active in their lives is the core of spiritual development.

6. **Reflection on prayer**

   The group might take half an hour or so to discuss various approaches of contemplative prayer. The facilitator may provide readings on contemplative prayer for discussion (see bibliography for some examples) or invite discussion of the group's experiences of contemplative prayer if they are practicing it alone at home. This is a time to explore the topic and to learn together.

7. **Centring prayer**

   The facilitator briefly explains guidelines for centring prayer:

   ❖ Choose a meaningful word as the symbol of your intention to consent to God's presence and action within, for example, love, shalom, abba, or peace. The choice is a personal one and may be changed from one time to another, but should be kept during any given prayer session.

   ❖ Sitting comfortably, with eyes closed, settle briefly and silently say the word. This is a symbol of your consent to God's presence and action within you.

   ❖ When you become aware of thoughts, return ever-so-gently to the word.

   ❖ At the end of the prayer period, remain in silence with eyes closed for a couple of minutes, to allow yourself to return to awareness of the group.

Before beginning the prayer time encourage participants to find a comfortable place to sit. Some may prefer, for example, an upright chair; others may prefer sitting on the floor and leaning against the wall. Contemplative prayer is not a form of relaxation, but attentive listening. Participants should be comfortable and try to keep their backs as straight as possible and their feet flat on the floor if seated in a chair.

Mark the beginning and the end of the prayer time with chimes, a bell, a singing bowl, or taped music. The advantage of using taped music is that the facilitator can easily participate in the prayer time without worrying about marking the end of the session. Meditation tapes are available for sale or you can make your own. (Record an appropriate piece of music on to a tape and then leave a period of silence—up to 30 minutes—before recording the music again. When the music begins the second time, it is an indication that the centring prayer time is coming to an end. You may want to begin with 10 minutes of silence and work your way up to 20-30 minutes.)

8. **Check-out**

Review the discussion of "Check-out" (Chapter 7, page 43). Some check-out questions might be:

❖ Is there something from your prayer experience that you would like to share with others?

❖ What one word describes how you feel after this prayer session?

❖ What image describes how you feel after this prayer session?

Keeping a journal is also a useful exercise after a contemplative prayer session.

Participants may simply wish to write down some of the feelings of the experience.

Another option might be to invite participants to choose a word that in some way symbolizes the session for them and write it down in the centre of the page. The participants can then write words relating to this core image in spoke-like fashion around it. The words should be allowed "to emerge" from the experience. They can later be used during personal prayer time at home as a way to reflect on what appears to be happening to their inner life as they experience God's presence within them.

Consider providing rough paper, such as coloured construction paper or watercolour paper, and art pastels, for each participant. Invite them to draw an image that emerges from their prayer experience. To stay connected to the heart experience of contemplative prayer, some participants may find it helpful to try drawing with their non-dominant hand. The emphasis is on finding ways to express inner experience and bring it closer to consciousness.

As part of the check-out, each participant might speak briefly about the word or image that they have written or created. Such sharing can help to enrich others' understanding of their own experience.

Note: The intention of contemplative prayer is to move toward a deeper openness to the Divine. The facilitator needs to ensure that any activities related with this form of prayer do not become overly analytical. This is a spiritual experience rather than one that is primarily intellectual.

8. **Closing**

It is important to have some sort of closing to bring the meeting to an end. The "Blessing of Light" (see Appendix 1) is an effective ritual to use as a closing for a contemplative prayer group.

9. **Quiet Time**

Allow for a short quiet time after the meeting ends so that participants have a chance to adjust to returning to the rest of their day.

Praying with Scripture

This method of prayer is also known as the African Bible reflection, the African model, or the Lambeth method. Praying with scripture is a very effective group spiritual exercise. Used over a period of time it has many benefits, such as:

❖ learning to listen more deeply to the scriptures

❖ learning to voice our own personal struggles with God's call

❖ learning to listen prayerfully and attentively to others

❖ learning to be comfortable with silence

❖ learning to pray for each other

❖ learning to respect our own and others' experiences of and responses to scripture

❖ learning to keep confidences

❖ learning to accompany each other on our faith journeys

Praying with Scripture: The Process

Description

The facilitator informs the participants about the method of the exercise:

❖ This is a reflection based on personal experience and not a study based on trying to come to a correct historical or theological understanding of the text.

❖ The text will be read three times, by three different people throughout the exercise (the same version of the text can be read each time or different version can be used).

❖ A period of deep silence follows each reading.

❖ What is shared in the group remains in the group.

❖ Participants can pass and not share verbally if they chose.

❖ Each person's reflections should be listened to and not commented upon by others. There is **no** discussion.

Part 1

The facilitator tells the group that they should listen for a word or phrase that catches their attention. One person reads the passage out loud. Everyone else listens without looking at the text. When the reader has finished reading, she or he also sets the text aside. Have at least one minute of silence.

The facilitator asks the participants to recall the word or phrase that emerged for them, and to share it with the group. There is no further explanation or discussion.

Part 2

In preparation for the second reading of the passage, the facilitator asks the group to listen for how the passage is speaking to their lives today. A second person reads the passage and all others listen. The reader sets the text aside when finished reading. Have at least three minutes of silence as the participants listen to discern where the passage connects with some part of their life. One by one, participants share their responses with no discussion.

Part 3

Before the third reading of the passage, the facilitator asks the group to listen to the passage with the following question in mind, "*From what I have heard and shared, how does God want me to be? What does God want me to do or perhaps not do this week? Or how does God want me to change?*" The facilitator also tells the group that, after the sharing time, each person will be asked to pray for the person on his or her left, in response to what that person shared.

A third person reads the passage while all others listen. The reader puts the text away. Have three to five minutes of silence as participants listen to the way the passage is speaking to them in terms of being, acting, changing.

The participants share their responses. They then join hands and take turns ...aying for the person on their left, going around the circle to the right. (In this way, the person who is praying has not just been prayed for. Receiving prayer can be an emotional experience.)

Conclude the session by saying the Lord's Prayer together.

Check-Out
Review the discussion of "Check-outs" Chapter 7, page 43. Also see above for the check-out process of contemplative prayer groups.

Exploring Prayer and Spiritual Practices Small Group

Some may wish to form a group that explores various ways to pray and different types of spiritual practices. Participants can then use these practices in other small groups or as part of their personal prayer life. Unlike the other prayer groups previously described, participants in this group do not concentrate on one practice but learn a few.

The group will have to decide how it is going to approach this task. Three of many possible options are:

1. The group may decide for covenant for eight weeks, learning six different prayer or spiritual practices, with the first meeting as an introduction and the last to bring closure to the covenant.

2. The group may decide to covenant for eight weeks, learning three different techniques, allowing for two weeks for each one, with the first meeting as an introduction and the last to bring closure to the covenant.

3. The group may decide to covenant for a much longer time, say for 14 weeks, and learn three techniques, allowing for four weeks for each and leaving the first meeting as an introduction and the last to bring closure to the commitment.

If the group decides to take the first option, the group activity part of the meetings might follow a format similar to this one:

Week One: Introduction
             Participants share some of their experiences of prayer.
Week Two: Participants learn about and practise contemplative prayer.
             (Develop the group covenant.)

Week Three: Participants learn about and practise Praying with Scripture.
Week Four: Participants learn about and practise intercessory prayer.
Week Five: Participants learn about and practise guided meditations.
Week Six: Participants learn about and practise walking prayers, or using a labyrinth.
Week Seven: Participants review what's been learned and practised.
Week Eight: Participants evaluate the small group session, bring the covenant to a close, and celebrate their time together.

Check-out
Consider the check-out examples for contemplative prayer offered above.

Chapter 12
Considering the Group's Ministry

Groups are encouraged to consider the way that the three aspects of ministry, ministry to the participants, to the faith community, the congregation and to the wider world relate to them. The question arises, how do group participants do this during their time together? Is this done on an ongoing basis, or is time taken at one of the meetings to think about this?

There are different ways to approach this. Each group will need to find the one that works best for it. One possibility is to have participants answer the questions below to help them to reflect on their group's ministry. Participants can do this individually, perhaps as part of the check-out, or at home after each meeting. If participants were able to do this after each meeting in writing, it would help to provide a journal of how they see the group's ministry unfolding.

Doing this exercise after each meeting may feel somewhat burdensome. The group may wish to do this once or twice during the life of the group. The group could then set aside a time during one of their final meetings to talk about what they have been experiencing. The group may be able to identify a particular experience or learning that it would like to share with the rest congregation. It may also be able to identify some activity which would lead to a new small group.

Ministry to the Individual

❖ What has been a blessing to me during this meeting?

❖ What has been a challenge?

❖ Did I experience any conflict within myself? If so, what was the conflict?

❖ Did I experience any conflict with anyone else? With whom? Is there something we need to resolve?

❖ Was I moved to tears at any time during the meeting? What could that mean?

❖ How did I sense God's presence during the meeting?

Ministry to the Faith Community/Congregation

❖ Did anything that occurred during the meeting have a direct relation to the life of the congregation?

❖ Did anything during the meeting challenge my feelings for, or relationship with, the congregation?

❖ What happened during the meeting that might be valuable to share with the rest of congregation?

❖ What might the group need from the congregation?

❖ How do I sense God's presence as I consider my relationship with the congregation?

Ministry to the Wider World

❖ Did anything that happened during the meeting call into question my life at home, at work, or with my community locally, nationally, or internationally?

❖ Did anything happen during the meeting to challenge my understanding of our congregation's relationship with the wider world?

❖ Do I feel moved to take on some action personally, with the group, or within the wider world?

❖ What questions did our spiritual practice raise about the group's or my relationship to the wider world?

❖ How do I sense God's presence as I consider my or the group's relationship with the wider world?

Appendix 1
Options for Openings, Check-Ins, Closings, and Check-Outs

Openings

A group may develop an opening that it uses each meeting or it may use a different one each time. Here are a few examples to help you get started or to inspire you to develop your own. Elements of various openings can be used to create new ones.

Keeping It Simple

Need:
Candle, matches

Process:
Light the candle: The facilitator lights candle the first week. Invite one of the participants to light the candle the next week. Try to find a different person to do this each meeting.

Prayer: The facilitator offers a gathering prayer of thanksgiving. For example:

> *Loving God, Holy Mystery*
> *We thank you for this day, with all of its blessings and challenges*
> *We are grateful for the opportunity to gather together in this group*
> *and to spend this time together.*
> *As we meet this evening, help us to be open to your gracious love so*
> *that in knowing you more deeply we may know ourselves and each*
> *other more deeply.*
> *Amen.*

Opening with Song

Need:

❖ Song sheets, hymn books, and/or an overhead projector and words of the song.

❖ Musical accompaniment is always good to have but not necessary.

Process:

❖ The group spends time singing songs members wish to sing. This can be done very informally.

❖ The group may decide to choose a "theme" song that it uses to indicate that the singing is coming to an end.

❖ The facilitator helps the group to centre by lighting a candle and saying a prayer.

Note: You might want to adjust your meeting's schedule so that there is enough time for your group to get enough singing in. If your group really likes to sing, you may want to start a small group ministry that focuses on singing!

A Ritual of Light and Water

Need:

❖ a large candle to represent the Spirit of God

❖ a bell, chimes, or a singing bowl (optional)

❖ a small floating candle for each participant

❖ matches

❖ large bowl with water in it

❖ prayer

❖ song, with words available for participants

Process:

❖ The facilitator calls group together by lighting the large candle, or ringing a bell, chimes, or singing bowl.

❖ The facilitator offers a prayer of thanksgiving and gathering.

❖ The group may wish to sing a song.

Each participant is invited to come up, one by one, take a small candle, light it from the large candle and place it into the bowl of water as a symbol of the individual spirit feed by the spirit of God and nurtured together in the waters of divine love.

❖ The facilitator offers a prayer of group unity and openness to God's love, for example:

> *Living God, whose spirit feeds ours,*
> *We come together to be open to your love and to your grace.*
> *We come together to be bathed in the waters of your love,*
> *A love that is at once nurturing and demanding*
> *As it asks us to live out of an ever deepening compassion*
> *So that justice and goodness are known in the world.*
> *Amen.*

Check-ins

Questions for Checking-in

The question could be very open and general, such as:

* How are you this evening?
* How have things been going since our last meeting?

The advantage of this type of question is that it lets people get what's on their minds out, allowing participants to be more fully present.

The question could be more focused on spiritual nurture such as:

* Where have you experienced God since we last met?
* For what have you felt gratitude since our last meeting? For what have you experienced a sense of regret?

For groups that want to be more intentional about having participants consider where God is active in their lives, one of the above questions could be asked after an initial check-in is finished.

The group might want to have its own talking stick (or stone, feather, etc.) to use for check-in. Only the person with the object speaks. The object can be passed around the circle from person to person, or after one person finishes speaking it is put on the worship table and when someone else is ready to speak she or he picks it up.

Activities for Check-in

* Have an assortment of different coloured or different shaped objects such as jelly beans, beads, buttons, shells, stones, etc. Ask participants to choose the one that best describes how they are feeling.
* Have some objects on the worship table such as a stone, flower, feather, shell, cross, etc. Ask participants to choose one that speaks to them and how they are feeling.
* From an assortment of pictures, such as photographs or magazine pictures, ask participants to choose one that best reflects how they are feeling.

Check-outs

Questions for Checking-out

❖ Is there a thought or a reflection that you would like to share?

❖ For what have you felt gratitude during the meeting?

❖ What you are taking with you from this meeting?

❖ What biblical passage reflects our time during the meeting?

❖ What image comes to mind as you reflect on the meeting?

The group might want to have its own talking stick (or stone, feather, etc.) to use for check-out. Only the person with the object speaks. The object can be passed around the circle from person to person, or after one person finishes speaking the object is put on the worship table and when someone else is ready to speak she or he picks it up.

Activities for Check-out

❖ Participants choose an object from the worship table that best reflects how they are feeling or what they are thinking.

❖ Participants take a moment to sit in silence and let a word or an image arise in their minds from the meeting that is meaningful to them. This could be a biblical image or anything else that emerges. Participants write the word down in the centre of a piece of paper. They then connect the word or image with an image or event that is related to their day-to-day life. The primary question here is, "Where is your faith leading you in your relationship with others, such as family, friends, colleagues, and strangers?" Participants can then share some of their insights with the group.

Closings

A group may develop a closing that it uses at each meeting or it may use a different one each time.

Here are a few examples to help you get started, or to inspire you to develop your own. Elements of various openings can be used to create new ones.

Close with a Prayer

The group gathers in a circle around or near the worship centre. The facilitator or another group member says a closing prayer.

Close with a Song

The group gathers in a circle around or near the worship centre and sings a song together. The facilitator or another group member says a closing prayer.

Gifts for the Journey

The facilitator invites each member of the group to name the gift or gifts that she or he needs from God for the days ahead. These could be, for example wisdom, strength, courage, patience, compassion, joy, humility, gratitude trust in self or trust in God.

After each participant names what they need the facilitator or another participant offers these requests to God and brings the prayer to a close.

A Blessing of Light

Participants gather around a central candle. The facilitator asks each participant to think of a gift that she or he needs from God for the days ahead. (See above, Gifts for the Journey.) One participant holds her or his hands over the candle, concentrating on the holiness of the Light of the world, God's love. The participant turns to the person on the left and raises her or his hands over that person's head. The person to be blessed names the gift she or he wishes to receive. Saying the person's name, and keeping a distance of a few inches, the person doing the blessing begins to slowly move her or his hands down the person's head, shoulders, and arms while all participants say together:
We bless you with the light of God's love. May you be filled with _____ (desired gift).

Participants continue around the circle until everyone has been blessed.

Appendix 2
Some Questions about Small Group Ministry

Is it possible to get "grouped out"?
Yes. One can be grouped out in the sense of belonging to too many groups and hence feeling overly busy, and in the sense that there may be times when one does not want to belong to any group. It is very important to be able to set personal boundaries, know when one is too involved, and be able to say "no" to belonging to a group.

How do you respond when people say, "There's way too much going on here!"
This sounds like a cry of desperation. Who is saying it? Why is there a problem? Are needs being meet by the congregation's busyness? Are problems being caused by the busyness? What are they? Why do people feel overwhelmed?

When busyness becomes a burden, life-denying rather than life-giving, it is a concern. People need to be encouraged to set their own limits raising such questions as: Am I taking on too much? What am I neglecting to belong to this group? Does it matter? What do I really need right now? The minister or the small group coordinator, if a congregation has one, needs to make it clear that belonging to more groups is not necessarily better.

What happens when too many groups are operating at the same time?
If the issue here is space, what are the alternatives? Do all the groups need to meet in the church? Are there other ways for people to meet? How can the groups involved find ways to negotiate the space?

What happens when the same people are in every group?
A basic premise of small group ministry is that groups form depending on the interests of the participants. It may be that some people have not heard the message that they should feel free to start a group based on their own interests. There is also the possibility that some people do not feel welcome to be part of a group. Is there something that is keeping people from participating?

What about having a small group ministry group for those who seldom or never attend congregational worship and don't intend to be part of the congregation?

Many congregations have groups that meet in the church building, but otherwise have nothing to do with the greater congregational life. If a congregation is comfortable sharing, or in some cases renting out its space, that's fine. These groups, however, should not be burdened with pressures of being small group ministry groups. They aren't.

If a group meets which sees itself loosely connected to the congregation but many or all of its participants do not connect with the congregation outside of the group, you cannot really force these people to be a small group ministry. The group could be invited to learn more about small group ministry; perhaps they will decide to incorporate some aspects into their life.

Some people don't participate in church groups. How do we prevent them from being ostracized?

The questions to be asked are, "Why are they being ostracized?" "Who is ostracizing them?" Is small group ministry being set up as the only way to develop spiritually and live faithfully? Or is it being presented as one way of being in community through which participants can develop spiritually and live more faithfully?

How do you deal with the assumption that, if you are not expressing your faith or prayer life in the small group context, it doesn't exist, or is somehow deficient?

If a congregation is taking this approach to small group ministry, there is a critical misunderstanding as to what small group ministry is all about. One's faith and spirituality develops in many ways. Coming together in community, large and small, is without a doubt a very important way. While the invitation to meet in small groups should be open, the stipulation that if one is not part of a group, one is not "spiritual" or "faithful" is simply wrong.

Are there any dangers of small group ministry we need to keep in mind?

A few dangers that can arise are:

❖ Groups can become cliques.

❖ Groups can take on a "group mentality." That is to say, if an idea or position comes from a few in a group, it implies that everyone thinks and feels the same way. Some may fear to challenge the group mentality. Others may find solace in it and become overly identified with it.

❖ Groups can see themselves as spiritually superior to other groups or to those who do not participate in groups.

❖ Small group ministry is seen as an end in itself and not as a way to nurture spirituality. People consequently feel that they must belong, but do not necessarily take the challenges related to spiritual growth seriously.

Do all groups in the congregation have to be small group ministry groups?
No. Groups may want to meet in some other manner.

Can other kinds of groups nurture participants' faith?
Yes, they can be. God's spirit works in and through us even when we are not aware of it. Small group ministry as spiritual nurture means that groups are consciously and intentionally developing the group experience as a way to nurture spirituality. Becoming more and more aware of God in and through our lives means that we can respond in more life-giving and healing ways for ourselves and for others.

But shouldn't we insist that all groups meet as small group ministry groups so that we become a congregation of small groups? Shouldn't we be adamant about this for their sakes and for the sake of the congregation?
No. Although it is certainly desirable that all groups take on their tasks as "holy work" and see the group time as an opportunity for spiritual nurture, this should not be mandated. Groups need to have the opportunity to learn about small group ministry but they also need to decide for themselves the best way to meet.

Will small group ministry solve all our congregation's woes?
It would certainly be a mistake to think that small group ministry is a sure-fire remedy for congregational woes. It is not a recipe to be followed step by step to guarantee success. It is better understood as a "vessel" that allows for things to happen. Since the things that are happening have to do with spiritual growth, nurturing faith, community building, and growing awareness of ministry, there are bound to be many challenges for those involved.

Small group ministry will probably create a new set of challenges for the congregation. The hope, however, is that as group participants learn to be in community and learn to listen to each other, to pray for each other, and to find common ground upon which to meet and carry out ministry, challenges will be addressed differently. That is to say, as issues arise they will be met prayerfully and in a spirit of wishing only the best for everyone involved as each challenge is viewed as a chance for spiritual growth, not as the opportunity to dismiss, or discredit others, but as the opportunity to become more deeply rooted in the Divine.

Bibliography

Works Cited

Chittister, Joan, *Living Well: Scriptural Reflections for Every Day* (Maryknoll, NY: Orbis, 2000).

Guenther, Margaret, *The Practice of Prayer* (Cambridge, MA: Cowley, 1998).

Nouwen, Henri, *The Life of the Beloved: Spiritual Living in a Secular World* (New York: Crossroad/Herder & Herder, 2002).

O'Donohue, John, *Anam Cara: A Book of Celtic Wisdom* (New York: HarperCollins, 1997).

Palmer, Parker J., *The Company of Strangers: Christians and the Renewal of America's Public Life* (New York: Crossroad, 1983).

Sinetar, Marsha, *The Mentor's Spirit: Life Lessons on Leadership and the Art of Encouragement* (New York: St. Martin's Press, 1998).

Thompson, Marjorie, *Soul Feast: An Invitation to the Christian Spiritual Life* (Louisville, KY: Westminster John Knox Press, 1995).

Welch, John, *Spiritual Pilgrims: Carl Jung and Teresa of Avila* (Mahwah, NJ: Paulist Press, 1982).

Selected Bibliography

The following selected bibliography is divided into two parts. The first part lists books related to small group ministry and spiritual nurture under the headings of Considering Spirituality, Leadership Development, Spiritual Growth for Congregations, Spiritual Practices, Small Group Ministry and Pastoral Care, and The Community Called Church. While these books have been listed to provide background material on small group ministry as spiritual nurture, they are also excellent material for small group study.

The second part lists books thematically that could be used for small group study under the following headings: Biblical Questions, Ecology, Faith Moved to Action, Forgiveness in a Broken World, Jesus, Interfaith Dialogue, Life After Death, Sexuality, Finding Our Way in Challenging Times, and Theology/God Talk.

The lists are by no means exhaustive. They are samplers of the vast material that is available. The books listed here are intended to encourage, to challenge, and to inspire. Many of these books could be included under a number of headings. Readers are encouraged to use the material as best suits their needs.

1. Books on Small Group Ministry and Spiritual Nurture

Considering Spirituality

O'Donohue, John, *Anam Cara*: A Book of Celtic Wisdom (New York: HarperCollins, 1997).

Friend, Jr., Howard E., *Recovering the Sacred Center: Church Renewal from the Inside Out* (Valley Forge, PA: Judson Press, 1998).

Synder, Mary Hembrow, ed., *Spiritual Questions for the Twenty-First Century* (Maryknoll, NY: Orbis Books, 2001).

O'Murchu, Diarmuid, *Reclaiming Spirituality: A New Spiritual Framework for Today's World* (New York: Crossroad, 2000).

Rupp, Joyce, and Mary Southard, art, *The Cosmic Dance: An Invitation to Experience Our Oneness* (Maryknoll, NY: Orbis Books, 2002).

Tindal, Mardi, *Soul Maps: A Guide to the Mid-Life Spirit* (Toronto: United Church Publishing House/Anglican Book Centre, 2000).

Weems, Renita, *Listening For God: A Minister's Journey Through Silence and Doubt* (New York: Touchstone Books, 2000).

Leadership Development

Allison Hahn, Celia, *Growing in Authority: Relinquishing Control, A New Approach to Faithful Leadership* (Bethesda, MD: Alban Publications, 1998).

Kirkpatrick, Thomas G., *Small Groups in the Church: A Handbook for Creating Community* (Bethesda, MD: Alban Publications, 1995).

Olsen, Charles M., *Transforming Church Boards Into Communities of Spiritual Leaders* (Bethesda, MD: Alban Publications, 1995).

Olsen, Charles and Ellen Morseth, *Selecting Church Leaders: A Practice in Spiritual Discernment* (Nashville: Upper Room Books, 2002).

Sinetar, Marsha, *The Mentor's Spirit: Life Lessons on Leadership and the Art of Encouragement* (New York: St. Martin's Press, 1998).

Turner, Nathan W., *Leading Small Groups: Basic Skills for Church and Community Organizations* (Valley Forge, PA: Judson Press, 1996).

Spiritual Growth for Congregations

Ackerman, John, *Spiritual Awakening: A Guide to Spiritual Life in Congregations* (Bethesda, MD: Alban Publications, 1995).

Allison Hahn, *Celia, Uncovering Your Church's Hidden Spirit* (Bethesda, MD: Alban Publications, 2001).

Meyer, Richard C., *One Anothering, Vol. 2, Building Spiritual Community in Small Groups* (Philadelphia: Innisfree Press, 1999).

Morris, Danny E. and Charles M. Olsen, *Discerning God's Will Together: A Spiritual Practice for the Church* (Bethesda, MD: Alban Publications, 1997).

Ware, Corrine, *Connecting to God: Nurturing Spirituality Through Small Groups* (Bethesda, MD: Alban Publications, 1998).

Ware, Corrine, *Discover Your Spiritual Type: A Guide to Individual and Congregational Growth* (Bethesda, MD: Alban Publications, 1997).

Spiritual Practices

Baldwin, Christina, *Life's Companion: Journal Writing as a Spiritual Quest* (New York: Bantam Books, 1991).

Brooke, Avery, *Healing in the Landscape of Prayer* (Cambridge, MA: Cowley Publications, 1996).

Carse, James P., *The Silence of God: Meditations on Prayer* (New York: HarperCollins, 1985).

Collins, Pat, *Prayer in Practice* (Maryknoll, NY: Orbis Books, 2001).

Curry, Helen, *The Way of the Labyrinth: A Powerful Meditation for Everyday Life* (New York: Penguin Compass, 2000).

Dossey, Larry, et al., *Healing Through Prayer: Health Practitioners Tell Their Story* (Toronto: Anglican Book Centre, 1999).

Gruff, Kent Ira, *Active Spirituality: A Guide for Seekers and Ministers* (Bethesda, MD: Alban Publications, 1993).

Gutierrez, Gustavo, *We Drink From Our Own Wells: The Spiritual Journey of a People* (Maryknoll, NY: Orbis Books, 2003).

Johnson, Robert A., *Inner Work: Using Dreams and Active Imagination for Personal Growth* (New York: Harper and Row, 1989).

Keating, Thomas, *Open Heart, Open Mind: The Contemplative Dimension of the Gospel* (New York: Continuum, 1997).

Keating, Thomas, *Invitation to Love: The Way of Christian Contemplation* (New York: Continuum, 2000).

Kelsey, Morton, *Dreams: A Way to Listen to God* (New York: Paulist Press, 1979).

Leckey, Dolores R., *Seven Essential for the Spiritual Journey* (New York: Crossroad, 1999).

Main, John, *Essential Writings* (Maryknoll, NY: Orbis Books, 2002).

Mathis, Rick, *Prayer-Centered Healing: Finding the God Who Heals* (Ligouri, MO: Ligouri Publications, 2000).

Moon, Sharon, *The Healing Oasis: Guided Meditations for Mind, Body and Soul* (Toronto: United Church Publishing House, 1998).

Moore, Thomas, *Care of the Soul: A Guide for Cultivating Depth and Sacredness in Everyday Life* (New York: HarperPerennial, 1994).

Myss, Caroline, *Anatomy of the Spirit: The Seven Stages of Power and Healing* (New York: Three Rivers Press, 1996).

Reininger, Gustave, ed., *Centering Prayer in Daily Life and Ministry* (New York: Continuum, 1998).

Rohr, Richard, *Everything Belongs: The Gift of Contemplative Prayer* (New York: The Crossroad Publishing, 1999).

Skinner Sawyers, June, *Praying with Celtic Saints, Prophets, Martyrs, and Poets* (Ashland, Ohio: Sheed & Ward, 2001).

Taylor, Barbara Erakko, *Silence: Making the Journey to Inner Quiet* (Philadelphia: Innis Free Press, 1997).

Thompson, Marjorie J., *Soul Feast: An Invitation to the Christian Spiritual Life*. Louisville, KY: Westminster John Knox Press, 1995).

Vest, Norvene, *Still Listening: New Directions in Spiritual Direction* (Harrisburg, PA: Morehouse Publishing, 2000).

Small Group Ministry and Pastoral Care

Hutchinson, Joyce, with prayers by Joyce Rupp, *May I Walk You Home? Courage and Comfort for Caregivers of the Very Ill* (Notre Dame, IN: Ave Maria Press, 1999).

Peel, Donald, *The Ministry of Healing: Team Visiting in Hospital and Home* (Toronto: Anglican Book Centre, 1980).

Stairs, Jean, *Listening for the Soul: Pastoral Care and Spiritual Direction* (Minneapolis: Fortress Press, 2000).

The Community Called Church

Cosby, Gordon, *Handbook for Mission Groups* (Waco, Texas: Word Books, 1975). (While now over 25 years old, this book by the founder of the Church of the Saviour in Washington D.C., is still very relevant today).

Hebblethwaite, Margaret, *Basic is Beautiful: Basic Ecclesial Communities from Third World to the First World* (London: HarperCollinsPublishers, 1993).

Leddy, Mary Jo, *Radical Gratitude* (Maryknoll, NY: Orbis Books, 2000).

Noe, K. Killian, *Finding Our Way Home* (Washington, DC: Servant Leadership Press, 2001).

2. Further Themes for Small Group Study
Biblical Questions

Borg, Marcus, *Reading the Bible Again for the First Time: Taking the Bible Seriously But Not Literally* (New York: HarperCollins Publishers, 2002).

Brown, Robert McAfee, *Unexpected News: Reading the Bible with Third World Eyes* (Philadelphia: The Westminster Press, 1984).

Fiorenza, Elisabeth Schussler, *Wisdom Ways: Introducing Feminist Biblical Interpretation* (Maryknoll, NY: Orbis Books, 2001).

Kadowaki, J.K., *Zen and the Bible* (Maryknoll, NY: Orbis Books, 2002).

Ringe, Sharon H. and Wes Howard-Brook, eds., *The New Testament – Introducing the Way of Discipleship* (Maryknoll, NY: Orbis Books, 2002).

Spong, John Shelby, *Liberating the Gospels: Reading the Bible with Jewish Eyes* (Scarborough: HarperCollins Canada, 1997).

Spong, John Shelby, *Rescuing the Bible from Fundamentalism: A Bishop Rethinks the Meaning of Scripture* (San Francisco: HarperSanFrancisco, 1992).

Torre, Miquel, A. de la, *Reading the Bible from the Margins* (Maryknoll, NY: Orbis Books, 2002).

Ecology

McFague, Sallie, *Super, Natural Christian: How We Should Love Nature* (Minneapolis: Fortress Press, 1997).

McFague, Sallie, *Life Abundant: Rethinking Theology and Economy for a Planet in Peril* (Minneapolis: Fortress Press, 2000).

Faith Moved to Action

Palmer, Parker J., *The Company of Strangers: Christians and the Renewal of America's Public Life* (New York: Crossroad, 1999).

Shore, Edith, *Lying Down with Lions: Building the Peaceable Kingdom – Helping Women Who Have Served Time in Prison and Building Healthy Communities* (Toronto: Inter-Church Working Group on Violence and Sexual Abuse, 2000).

Soelle, Dorothee, *Against the Wind: Memoirs of a Radical Christian* (Minneapolis: Augsburg Fortress, 1999).

Forgiveness in a Broken World

Arnold, Johann Christoph, *Why Forgive?* (Maryknoll: Orbis Books, 2003).

Jenco, Lawrence Martin, O.S.M., *Bound to Forgive: The Pilgrimage to Reconciliation of a Beirut Hostage* (Notre Dame, IN: Ave Maria Press, 1995).

Linn, Dennis, Sheila Fabricant Linn, & Matthew Linn, *Don't Forgive Too Soon: Extending the Two Hands that Heal* (New York: Paulist Press, 1997).

Minow, Martha, *Between Vengeance and Forgiveness: Facing History After Genocide and Mass Violence* (Boston: Beacon Press, 1999).

Shults, F. L., *The Faces of Forgiveness: Searching for Wholeness and Salvation* (Ada, MI: Baker Book House, 2003).

Tutu, Desmond, *No Future Without Forgiveness* (New York: Doubleday Publishing, 2000).

Jesus

Borg, Marcus, *Meeting Jesus Again for the First Time: The Historical Jesus and the Heart of Contemporary Faith* (San Francisco: Harper SanFrancisco, 1994).

Borg, Marcus and N.T. Wright, *The Meaning of Jesus: Two Visions* (New York: HarperCollins, 2000).

Gateley, Edwina & Robert Lentz, *Christ in the Margins* (Maryknoll, NY: Orbis Books, 2003).

Haight, Roger, Jesus, *Symbol of God* (Maryknoll, NY: Orbis, 1999).

Kuster, Volker, *The Many Faces of Jesus Christ* (Maryknoll, NY: Orbis, 1999).

Nolan, Albert, *Jesus Before Christianity* (Maryknoll, NY: Orbis Books, 2001).

Soares-Prabhu, George M., *The Dharma of Jesus* (Maryknoll, NY: Orbis Books, 2003).

Taussig, Hal, *Jesus Before God: The Prayer Life of the Historical Jesus* (Santa Rosa, CA: Polebridge Press, 1999).

Wessels, Cletus, *Jesus in the New Universe Story* (Maryknoll, NY: Orbis, 2003).

Interfaith Dialogue

Armstrong, Karen, *Battle for God: Fundamentalism in Judaism, Christianity, and Islam* (Scarborough: Random House, 2001).

Armour, Sr., Rollin, *Islam, Christianity, and the West: A Troubled History* (Maryknoll, NY: Orbis Books, 2002).

Ellis, Marc H., *Unholy Alliance: Religion and Atrocity in Our Time* (Minneapolis: Fortress Press, 1997).

Gorder, A. Christian van, *No God But God: A Path to Muslim-Christian Dialogue on God's Nature* (Maryknoll, NY: Orbis Books, 2003).

Scott, Susan L., ed., *Stories in my Neighbour's Faith: Narratives from World Religions in Canada* (Toronto: United Church Publishing House, 1999).

Life After Death

Arnold, Johann Christoph, *Be Not Afraid: Overcoming the Fear of Death* (Maryknoll, NY: Orbis Books, 2002).

Barr, James, *The Garden of Eden and the Hope of Immortality* (Minneapolis: Fortress Press, 1992).

Harpur, Tom, *Life After Death* (Toronto: McClelland & Stewart, 1991).

Kung, Hans, *Eternal Life: Life After Death as a Medical, Philosophical and Theological Problem* (New York: Doubleday, 1985).

Lackey, Douglas P., *God, Immortality, Ethics: A Concise Introduction to Philosophy* (Belmont, CA: Wadsworth Publishing Co., 1990).

Sawicki, Marianne, *Seeing the Lord: Resurrection and Early Christian Practices* (Minneapolis: Fortress Press, 1994).

Spong, John Shelby, *Resurrection: Myth or Reality?* (Scarborough: HarperCollins Canada, 1995).

Sexuality

Dessaix, Robert, *A Mother's Disgrace* (New York: HarperCollins Publishers, 1994).

Mollenkott, Virginia Ramey, *Omnigender: A Trans-religious Approach* (Cleveland, Ohio: The Pilgrim Press, 2002).

McCall Tigert, Leanne, *Coming Out Through Fire: Surviving the Trauma of Homophobia* (Cleveland, Ohio: United Church Press, 1999).

Spong, John Shelby, *Living in Sin? A Bishop Rethinks Sexuality* (Scarborough: Zondervan Publishing House, 1990).

Finding Our Way in Challenging Times

Cejka, Mary Ann & Thomas Bamat, eds., *Artisans of Peace: Grassroots Peacemaking among Christian Communities* (Maryknoll, NY: Orbis Books, 2003).

Chittister, Joan, *Scarred by Struggle, Transformed by Hope* (Grand Rapids, MI.: William B. Eerdmans, 2003).

Davis, Patricia with Dianna Ortiz, *The Blindfold's Eyes: My Journey from Torture to Truth* (Maryknoll, NY: Orbis Books, 2002).

Ellis, Marc H., *Unholy Alliance: Religion and Atrocity in Our Time* (Minneapolis: Fortress Press, 1997).

Hillman, James, *The Soul's Code: In Search of Character and Calling* (NewYork: Warner Books, 1997).

Howard-Brook, Wes, *The Church Before Christianity* (Maryknoll, NY: Orbis Books, 2001).

Mananzan, Mary John et al eds., *Women Resisting Violence: Spirituality for Life* (Maryknoll, NY: Orbis Books, 1996).

Smith-Christopher, Daniel L., ed., *Subverting Hatred: The Challenge of Nonviolence in Religious Traditions* (Maryknoll: Orbis Books, 1998).

Soelle, Dorothee, *Suffering* (Minneapolis: Augsburg Fortress, 1975).

Suchocki, Marjorie H., *The Fall to Violence: Original Sin in Relational Theology* (New York: Continuum Publishing Company, 1995).

Taylor, James, *Sin: A New Understanding of Virtue And Vice* (Kelowna: Northstone Publishing, 1997).

Vanier, Jean, *The Broken Body: Journey to Wholeness* (London: Darton, Longman and Todd, 1988).

Walters, Kerry, *Jacob's Hip: Finding God in an Anxious Age* (Maryknoll, NY: Orbis Books, 2003).

Theology/God Talk

Borg, Marcus, *The God We Never Knew: Beyond Dogmatic Religion to a More Authentic Contemporary Faith* (Scarborough: HarperCollins Canada, 1997).

Borg, Marcus and Ross Mackenzie, eds., *God at 2000* (Harrisburg: Morehouse Group, 2000).

Fox, Matthew, *Original Blessing* (Santa Fe: Bear & Company, 1983).

Harpur, Tom, *Would You Believe? Finding God Without Losing Your Mind* (Toronto: McClelland & Stewart, 1996).

Knitter, Paul F., *Introducing Theologies of Religions* (Maryknoll, NY: Orbis Books, 2002).

Langford, Jeremy, *God Moments: Why Faith Really Matters to a New Generation* (Maryknoll, NY: Orbis Books, 2001).

O'Murchu, Diarmuid, *Evolutionary Faith: Rediscovering God in Our Great Story* (Maryknoll, NY: Orbis Books, 2002).

Rieger, Joerg, *God and the Excluded; Visions and Blindspots in Contemporary Theology* (Minneapolis: Fortress Press, 2000).

Weems, Renita, *Listening For God: A Minister's Journey Through Silence and Doubt* (New York: Touchstone Books, 2000).

About the Author

Anne Martin is program staff with the Faith Formation and Education Unit of the General Council Offices of The United Church of Canada. Her areas of work include Small Group Ministry, Ministry with Men, and Ministry with Women. Anne is editor of the United Church's women's publication *Women's Concerns*.